Breaking Free
Through God's Promises

A
22-Day Devotional

Dysfunction

to
Function

Includes Psalm 119
&
Personal Testimonies

Breaking Free
Through God's Promises

A
22-Day Devotional

Dysfunction

to
Function

If You Want to Break Any Habit
You Must Change and Do things Different!

Elijah/Prophetic Trumpet Publishers
Debrh33@icloud.com

Copyright 2018-Tonja Peters
ISBN 9781984258885

Acknowledgment

A special thank you to my husband Ken for believing in me to accomplish anything that the Lord would put in front of me. I am the woman of God today, because of you leading me to the Lord Jesus Christ, who is the Author and the Finisher of my faith!

Thank you, Fawn Parish, for your gracious and loving suggestions for this devotional. And to Frank "Cyrus" McCormack Jr. with The Vision Publishers for helping me to finalize this project! I couldn't have finished this without the generosity of your time and commitment.

Prayer Request and Revelation of Hebrews 4:12

Hebrews 4:12 For the Word of God is living and powerful, and sharper than any two-edged sword, piercing even to the division of soul and spirit, and of joints and marrow, and is a discerner of the thoughts and intents of the heart.

September 16, 2016

Mom: *I'm sending a prayer request for my son. He was on the streets and shooting up meth and heroine and got very suicidal when my husband's friend reached out to help him in Los Angeles. He put himself into a psych ward. Then asked for help and was put into detox and a 30-day treatment program. He gets out today and is going into a Sober Living Home in North Hollywood. He expressed to us yesterday that he doesn't feel he's ready and he still feels the desire to do drugs. Please pray for a miracle.*

My response: *Praying for miracle workings!!!! Keep us posted. We are not far from North Hollywood. As I was praying for your son, I started praying that God would heal his heart. I declare emotional stability!!!*

October 7, 2016

Mom: *I want to keep you both updated on my son. He decided to leave the sober living home, and I haven't heard from him since. We are holding on to the words and promises spoken over him. I had a dream that I was telling you both this and Apostle Ken's response was to remember what the Lord said. So that is what we are doing. Thank you for your continued prayers, love and support.*

My response: *I'm sorry!! We are in agreement with God's promises for his life!!!*

Mom: *Thank you!!! Amen.*

October 19, 2016

Mom: *Praise God, our son is back in detox!*

My response: *Thank you, Lord! Continuing to Pray!! We need spiritual insight into how to pray against this type of drug addiction!*

Mom: Yes, I agree. I will definitely be praying, let me know if you get anything.

My response: Will do, I was just having a conversation about this horrific epidemic.

Mom: I was watching a program on TV about a new agenda in the prisons, which will allow them to give a prescription injection that actually blocks the cravings of many different drugs.

My response: Do you think it is long-term or temporary?

Mom: I think it gives them enough time to get it out of their system physically and especially the bones. I hear that the drugs linger in the bones for at least a year. There are other things they also do like counseling, therapy, and one on one advising.

October 20, 2016

My response: Good morning! Often the Holy Spirit will wake me with insights and revelation for things that I am walking through. After you shared about heroin being in the bones for up to a year. I woke up with this scripture; Hebrews 4:12 - The Word of God is sharper than any two-edged sword, piercing even to the joints and marrow, and is a discerner of the thoughts, and intentions of the heart. The Word of God meditated on will change the mind and even go into the joints and marrow!!!! Keep reminding your son of scriptures that the Holy Spirit gives you! Keep speaking and declaring Gods promises over him.

Mom: Amen, I will share this scripture with him, and I will be praying it over him!

June 12, 2017

My Response: Good Morning Friend! Thinking and praying for your son often! How has he been doing? FYI: since I started praying for your son and recovering from my broken leg (in which I had to deal with trauma and getting drugs out of my system). I wrote a devotional on Psalms 119. I felt like the Lord has shown me that this will be able to help those bound in addictions who desire to be healed. I wanted to share this with you because the inspiration came through praying for your son. Please pray that I can complete this project and get it into the right hands. Feeling led to give it to rehabilitation centers.

Mom: *Wow! That is so awesome. I will definitely be praying for you! Open the doors that no man can shut Lord!! Our son is doing good. He's living with the original Pastor that first started helping him. He is being discipled by him. He has him in devotions every morning; he has a job and is working on getting a car right now. He sounds and looks really good. But, definitely still needs prayer covering. Thank you for your love and prayer shield, there's nothing more precious than knowing he's covered in prayer.*

Table of Contents

Table of Contents

To the Reader,

In February of 2004, my family was driving southbound on the 101 Freeway in Nipomo, California. We were on our way home from church when a drunk driver hit our vehicle. The driver T-boned us hitting on my husband Ken and our daughter Candice's side of the SUV. We rolled several times, and the primary area of damage was on mine and our daughter Rachel's side of the vehicle.

That night, after they took the Jaws of Life to cut me out of the car, I was placed in the ambulance. While they began cutting my clothes off, I asked the Lord: "What is going on? Where are YOU?" He responded to me "I AM MAKING ALL THINGS NEW." I was not able to see it right away, in fact, it was after going through what felt like the darkest hour of my soul that I could even sense His Presence again. To this day, His Words that night have stayed close to my heart. I have embraced and continue to embrace the healing process for my life. This is a day, to day journey with my loving Savior.

Ken's injuries were minimal, pain in his hip, and a scratch on his hand. Candice had scrapes across her face with a little nick out of her nose. Rachel had somehow been ejected from the vehicle and was found a half of a football field away from us. To this day it is still unexplainable, with how her little body went through one of the windows. Her injuries were a compound right leg fracture, scrapes that covered her entire lower back, and a punctured spleen. My head was scalped above my left ear from the back to the front; My arm was broken in 2 places and shattered at the elbow. Almost all of my ribs were broken, which caused a lung to be punctured; My neck and back were fractured at 7 different vertebrae's.

Our family came through all of those injuries supernaturally! Within days, you couldn't tell that Candice had been in the wreck. Rachel's spleen had healed – never heard of before. And even in the midst of all of my injuries and multiple surgeries, the recovery was supernatural. The only thing that remained was the unseen wound's that scarred me internally – P.T.S.D. Post Trauma Stress Disorder. The Doctor that I saw explained to me that because my childhood was so traumatic, that when I recovered from all the injuries I suffered (including a brain injury) that my body did not know how to fight off the emotional trauma that I sustained.

Because I am a believer in the Lord Jesus Christ and the power of His written Word. I embraced the process of healing for my body, mind, (soul), and spirit. This was a drawn-out process, not just physically but emotionally and spiritually as well. My personality also changed dramatically. My daughter Candice had told me several times, "I wish I had my mom back."

Now, skipping ahead to September 4, 2016, twelve years later. My husband and I were visiting some friends in Maple Valley, Washington. In their backyard, they had a rope swing attached to a Zip Line. The day was so beautiful, as the sun shined upon the greenness of that valley, making the swing that was strung between hundreds of maple trees, so inviting, we took turns swinging on it. I wanted to go a second time, but this time, I was encouraged to jump off in the valley, instead of the place I had gotten onto the swing. As I jumped off, I landed on my left leg at an angle and sustained a compound fracture (yes the bone came out of my leg). I immediately put pressure on the swelling, not realizing that I was pushing on the bone that was coming out of my leg. I was able to set my own bone back into place.

So now, I was experiencing another traumatic event in my life. At first, I was so encouraged to be getting some rest from our busy schedule, even though I was a little restricted by my leg. After a couple of months, my husband says to me "Tonja, I don't think you are getting what the Lord wants for you during this time." So the next day, during my morning devotion, I began to ask the Lord what He required of me during this period. Immediately I dove into Psalm 119. In my mind, I was thinking, time is on my side; I have lots of it right now so I can study out Psalm 119. You see, I would read Psalms and Proverbs every morning, but when I would get to Psalm 119, I would pass it over because it was so long, the longest chapter in the Bible, to be exact.

I embraced a journey that has changed me from the inside out! As I studied Psalms 119, I was able to mine out nuggets of Truth from God's Promises that are transforming my mind, my heart, and my soul. The trauma that I sustained from breaking my leg caused the symptoms of PTSD to rise up again. As I studied this Psalm, the Holy Spirit would give me peace, and keep my mind focused on the TRUTH of Gods promises instead of the flood of lies that the enemy would say to me.

I believe that if a man or woman would take God's Word on a daily basis, and allow the Holy Spirit to transform and purify **your mind** and **heart**. That this would keep you from the wickedly evil plots of hell, which try to ensnare you and want to destroy you from the inside out.

Mark 7:14-23 When He had called all the multitude to Himself, He said to them, "Hear Me, everyone, and understand: There is nothing that enters a man from outside which can defile him; but the things which come out of him, those are the things that defile a man. If anyone has ears to hear, let him hear!"

*When He entered a house away from the crowd, His disciples asked Him concerning the parable. So He said to them, "Are you thus without understanding also? Do you not perceive that whatever enters a man from outside cannot defile him, because it does not enter his heart but his stomach, and is eliminated, thus purifying all foods?" And He said, "What comes out of a man, that defiles a man. For from within, out of the **heart of men**, proceed evil **thoughts**, adulteries, fornications, murders, thefts, covetousness, wickedness, deceit, lewdness, an evil eye, blasphemy, pride, and foolishness. All these evil things come from within and defile a man."(NKJV)*

My prayer for you is that whatever state of mind that you are in, that you would embrace the journey that God has for you and hide His Word in your heart. Let His Word transform you into His image. Our heavenly Father never intended for us to go through pain and suffering. But He knew that we would have to face trials and even some devastating experiences. This is why He sent His only Son to die on the cross for you and me. He wanted to make sure that we could find our way to Him (the original plan). Our God longs to be with us, and for us to desire to be with Him. And through His written Word we can do so, here on this earth. And even in the midst of everything, we can still experience a taste of eternity.

In this devotional, I have shared personal experiences, trials, traumas, and testimonies of how I was able to overcome. In Revelations 12:11 it says, "And they overcame him by the blood of the Lamb and the word of their testimony; and they loved not their lives into death."

I have found that my path to overcoming the strongholds that the enemy has thrown at me is by continually sharing my testimony every time God brings me through a trial or a trauma. Each time I share, I could feel God's Light shining ever so brightly into the dark places of shame, fear, and even every place the enemy would try to keep me bound in. God's Light would destroy Satan's grip on my life, and also bring growth and healing to others. I pray that in whatever battle you are facing, that you would embrace the process of real victory through the path of God's Word, genuinely hiding His Promises in your heart.

Tonja Peters,

*"When you move from the place of chaos
and confusion,
You're able to embrace the Life of The King
And His Kingdom"*

Introduction

This 22-day devotional includes Psalm 119, and personal testimonies from my life that are designed in such a way, that if you take each day and commit it to meditation, you will be changed. You may also use this study as a weekly bible study taking 1 Day each week to come together in a small group and discuss the revelation that the Holy Spirit reveals. Taking the time to read each scripture and taking your times of reflection to deep thought and meditation for what the Holy Spirit reveals. The slower process seems to be more effective for an individual with a busy lifestyle.

I believe that you can turn your life around from any addiction, trauma, or mental disease through the transformation process that comes through the Word of God! It has been said that it takes 21 days to break a bad habit. I believe that if any person would consider this 22-day Devotional while going through their recovery process, that the Holy Spirit would touch you. I believe that if you commit your mind, heart, and spirit to the transforming work of The Lord, and allow His Word to renew you, that you would indeed be set free, healed, and delivered by the renovating work of the Word of God. This will take a full *commitment and discipline* on your part to do what you read. So allow the Word of God to transform your mind and bring to your heart the healing and deliverance process that the Lord has for you; allow his restoration to do its perfect work.

I know this works because I used to be a drug addict and a drunk, and when I surrendered to the Lord with my whole heart, he delivered me and set me free. But you have to know that this only came with my complete surrender, and by releasing forgiveness to ALL who had wronged me. Yes, this can be painful, but just like any surgery; God brings grace and supernatural healing to get you through to the other side. Remember that it is God who does the work, not we in and of ourselves. All He desires from us is the cooperation of obedience to do His WILL. Our surrender, plus obedience, brings His benefits, healing, and FULL recovery. THE CHOICE IS YOURS!

Now, as the children of Israel climbed the steps up to the temple, they were instructed to sing the Psalms; God knew what He was doing. For there are 22 letters in the Hebrew alphabet, and Psalm 119 contains 22 units of 8 verses each. Each of the 22 sections is given to a letter of the Hebrew alphabet, and each section begins with that letter. This style of writing is provided to **aid** your ability in memorizing and hiding God's Word in your heart. To help you to further your study I have also included supporting scriptures that point to God's written revelation of each verse.

Psalm 119 glorifies God and His Word. It refers to Scripture over and over again, and the Psalm is amazing for how often it refers to God's Promises. The author of Psalm 119 is unnamed; commentators universally say it is a Psalm of David, which he composed throughout his entire life. Other commentators believe and often say that it is post-exilic, coming from the days of Nehemiah or Ezra. If it were important, God would have preserved the name of David to this Psalm. No matter who wrote it, it was likely written over some period of time and later compiled because there is not a definite flow of thought from the beginning of the Psalm to the end. The sections and verses are not like a chain, where one link is connected to the other, but like a string of pearls where each pearl has equal, but independent value.

David was a man after God's heart, and I believe that there is a key in Psalm 119:164 for finding our Father's heart by praising Him **throughout** every day. Truly stopping what we are regularly doing to center in on the Father. *Psalms*

119:164 says: **Seven times a day I praise You, because of Your righteous judgments.**

Now combine 2 Peter 1:1-11 and Galatians 5:16-26 with the study of Psalm 119 and **apply them to your life.** Do what it says, and you'll walk in the freedom that our Lord Jesus planned for you to live in for the rest of your life!

2 Peter 1:1-11 Simon Peter, a bondservant and apostle of Jesus Christ, to those who have obtained like precious faith with us by the righteousness of God and Savior Jesus Christ:

Grace and peace be multiplied to you in the knowledge of God and of Jesus our Lord, as His divine power has given to us all things that pertain to life and godliness, through the knowledge of Him who called us by glory and virtue, by which we have been given to us exceedingly great and precious promises, that through these you may be partakers of the divine nature, having escaped the corruption that is in the world through lust.

But also for this very reason, giving all diligence, add to your faith virtue, to virtue knowledge, to knowledge self-control, to self-control perseverance, to perseverance godliness, to godliness brotherly kindness, and to brotherly kindness love. For if these things are yours and abound you will be neither barren nor unfruitful in the knowledge of our Lord Jesus Christ. For he who lacks these things is shortsighted, even to blindness, and has forgotten that he was cleansed from his old sins.

Therefore, brethren, be even more diligent to make your call and election sure, for if you do these things, you will never stumble; for so an entrance will be supplied to you abundantly into the everlasting kingdom of our Lord and Savior Jesus Christ.

Galatians 5:16-26 *I say then: Walk in the Spirit, and you shall not fulfill the lust of the flesh. For the flesh lusts against the Spirit, and the Spirit against the flesh; and these are contrary to one another, so that you do not do the things you wish. But if you are led by the Spirit, you are not under the law.*

Now the works of the flesh are evident, which are; adultery, fornication, uncleanness, lewdness, idolatry, sorcery, hatred, contentions, jealousies, outbursts of wrath, selfish ambitions, dissensions, heresies, envy, murders, drunkenness, revelries, and the like of which I tell you beforehand, just as I also told you in time past, that those who practice such things will not inherit the kingdom of God.

But the fruit of the Spirit is love, joy, peace, longsuffering, kindness, goodness, faithfulness, gentleness, self-control. Against such, there is no law. And those who are Christ's have crucified the flesh with its passions and desires. If we live in the Spirit, let us also walk in the Spirit. Let us not become conceited, provoking one another, envying one another.

DAY 1

Seek Him With Your Whole Heart

Psalm 119:1-8
ALEPH
(Pronounced "ah-lef")

Blessed are the undefiled in the way,
Who walk in the law of the Lord!
Blessed are those who keep His testimonies,
Who seek Him with the whole heart!
They also do no iniquity;
They walk in His ways.
You have commanded us
To keep Your precepts diligently.
Oh, that my ways were directed
To keep Your statutes!
Then I would not be ashamed,
When I look into all Your commandments.
I will praise You with uprightness of heart,
When I learn Your righteous judgments
I will keep Your statutes;
Oh, do not forsake me utterly!

1

The Support Group

In 1989 I had attended a support group for recovering alcoholics and drug addicts. As I listened to the testimonies of several individuals, I realized that my testimony was different than the others. I couldn't understand why many of them would say, "I only slipped a couple times," or "this time I am 30 days clean." You see I was set free from drugs and alcoholism, and I remember the night so well: I had been invited to a bible study, and at the end of the study the Singles Pastor (now my husband) asked me, "Would you like to be filled with the Holy Spirit?" I said sure. I had just visited my dad the previous weekend, and he had prayed for me to receive, but nothing happened...so I thought I am going to try this again.

That night I *released forgiveness* to those who had hurt, abandoned, and rejected me. I received the power to overcome every obstacle that would come my way. I have never turned back to that lifestyle, and have now walked in the freedom of that power for 32 years.

Later, as I was pondering my life, "I asked myself why was I different?" I had asked my husband, "How come, I didn't struggle the way these individuals have?" His response to me was: "You loved God, more than the sin, and the drugs that bound you." For now thirty-two years I still think about my recovery, especially when I have gone through trials and difficult times. I have found that my love for my beautiful Savior, who saved me from a life of destruction, causes me to overcome every obstacle that the enemy would bring my way. He is beautiful beyond comprehension and greater than the drugs and alcoholism that was dragging me straight to the pit of hell. **Psalm 119:2**

Supporting Scriptures

Psalm 128:1 Blessed is everyone **who fears the Lord**, who walks in His ways.

Psalm 111: 10 The fear of the Lord is the beginning of wisdom; A good understanding have all those who do His commandments. His praise endures forever.

Ezekiel 11:19-20 Then I will give them one heart, and I will put a new spirit within them, and take the stony heart out of their flesh, and give them a heart of flesh, that they may walk in My statutes and keep My judgments and do them; and they shall be My people, and I will be their God.

Micah 4:2 Many nations shall come and say, Come, and let us go up to the mountain of the Lord, To the house of the God of Jacob; He will teach us His ways, And we shall walk in His paths." For out of Zion the law shall go forth, and the Word of the Lord from Jerusalem.

Deuteronomy 6:5 You shall **love the Lord your God with all your heart,** with all your soul, and with all your strength.

Deuteronomy 10: 12 And now, Israel, what does the Lord your God require of you, but to fear the Lord your God, to walk in all His ways and to love Him, to serve the Lord your God with all your heart and with all your soul.

Deuteronomy 11:13-14 And it shall be that if you earnestly obey My commandments which I command you today, to love the Lord your God and serve Him with all your heart and with all your soul, then I will give you the rain for your land in its season.....

Deuteronomy 13:1-4 If there arises among you a prophet or a dreamer of dreams, and he gives you a sign or a wonder,

3

*and the sign or the wonder comes to pass, of which he spoke to you, saying, "Let us go after other gods"- which you have not known-"and let us serve them," you shall not listen to the words of that prophet or that dreamer of dreams, for the Lord your God is testing you to know whether you love the Lord your God with all your heart and with all your soul. You shall walk after the Lord your God and fear Him, and keep His commandments and **obey His voice**; you shall serve Him and hold fast to Him.*

1 John 3:9 Whoever has been born of God does not sin, for His seed remains in him; and he cannot sin, because he has been born of God.

1 John 5:18 There is no fear in love, but perfect love casts out fear because fear involves torment. But he who fears has not been made perfect in love.

Key Word Definition

Undefiled: a. Not defiled; not polluted; not vitiated. (Definition of vitiated: depraved; rendered impure; rendered defective and void.)

Strong's Concordance: taw-meem' H8552; entire (literally, figuratively or morally): also (as noun) integrity, truth:- without blemish, complete, full, perfect, sincerely (-ity), sound, without spot, undefiled, upright (-ly), whole.

Total KJV Occurrences: 91

4

A Time of Reflection

Ask yourself, "Are there things in my life that I love more than the Lord?" Be honest with yourself.

_____

_____

_____

_____

_____

_____

_____

_____

_____

_____

Can you commit to putting the Lord first in your life?

Prayer of Repentance

Father, I ask You to forgive me of all my sins, I thank You that You sent your Son to die for me and my sins and that Your perfect blood was shed for me to wash and purge me of ALL my iniquity. This day I choose to put You first in my life and to forgive everyone who has sinned against me and caused me pain. I release forgiveness to everyone (identify), and I release all pain to you Lord.

I thank You for healing my heart, my mind, and physical body. Thank You for giving me the grace and ability to walk in real salvation and freedom that is promised to me. I ask Lord that You would complete the work that You have begun in me this day. I thank You for it! In Jesus Name, I pray, Amen. **John 3:16**

DAY 2

Your Word
I Have Hidden in My Heart

Psalm 119:9-16
BETH
(Pronounced beht)

How can a young man cleanse his way?
By taking heed according to Your Word;
With my whole heart I have sought You;
Oh, let me not wander from Your commandments!
Your Word I have hidden in my heart,
That I might not sin against You.
Blessed are You, O Lord!
Teach me Your statutes.
With my lips I have declared
All the judgments of Your mouth.
I have rejoiced in the way of Your testimonies,
As much as in all riches.
I will **meditate** on Your precepts,
And contemplate Your ways.
I will delight myself in Your statutes;
I will not forget Your Word.

I Was Determined

Shortly after I committed my life to the Lord Jesus Christ, our Pastor's mom encouraged me to read the bible all the way through. She gave me a yearly plan to do so. So I started this journey to read my bible in one year. Although I found that with the challenges of motherhood, three little ones at home, and working a part-time job, that I was unable to maintain my daily reading. I became discouraged, but I would start again at the beginning of every New Year. This went on for several years. January 1st I would begin, by March, I would be so far behind, I would give up. But by year 3, I was determined, I told myself, "I don't care how far behind I get, I am going to finish what I have started!" Well, I did not finish in 1 year, but I did not give up, it took me three years to read it all the way through from beginning to end.

God gave me a love for His Word during this season of my life. Taking the time to hide it in my heart became very transforming! My lack of education didn't matter as I allowed God's Word to transform me.

I genuinely believe that if you hide God's Word in your heart, and meditate on His promises continually, He will keep you blameless. He will cover you, and cause you to rise above every circumstance! Even taking what the enemy has meant for harm in your life and turning it around, allowing you to use it as a testimony to those who will hear.

Supporting Scriptures

2 Chronicles 15:15 And all Judah rejoiced at the oath, for they had sworn with all their heart and sought Him with all their soul; and He was found by them, and the Lord gave them rest all around.

Psalms 37:30-31 The mouth of the righteous speaks wisdom, and his tongue talks of justice. The law of his God is in his heart; none of his steps shall slide.

*Psalm 34:11 Come, you children, listen to me; I will teach you **the fear of the Lord**.*

*Psalms 1:1-3 Blessed is the man who walks not in the counsel of the ungodly, nor stands in the path of sinners, nor sits in the seat of the scornful; But his delight is in the law of the Lord, and in His law he **meditates** day and night. He shall be like a tree planted by the rivers of water, that brings forth its fruit in its season, whose leaf also shall not wither; and whatever he does shall prosper.*

Key Word Definition

Hidden: Concealed; placed in secrecy, unseen.

Strong's Concordance: H6845 tsaw-fan' A primitive root; to hide (by covering over); by implication to hoard or reserve; figuratively to deny; specifically (favorably) to protect, (unfavorably) to lurk; - esteem, hide (-den one, self) lay up, lurk (be set) privily, (keep) secret (-ly, place).

Total KJV Occurrences: 32

8

A Time of Reflection

Ask yourself: What do I spend time thinking about the most?
And what about my thought life needs to change?

_____

_____

_____

_____

_____

_____

_____

_____

Can you commit your mind to think differently, and do as
David did centering, and praising the Lord 7 times a day?
Psalms110: 164

_____

_____

_____

_____

_____

_____

_____

_____

_____

_____

Prayer of Confession

Father, I confess that I need You, You are my Lord, I believe with my whole heart that You died for my sins and was resurrected and now sit at the right hand of the Father. This day I choose to walk out my salvation by sharing what You have done for me. I ask that You give me the ability to articulate Your heart with others, that they may see who You are, and experience an authentic touch of Your Spirit. In Your precious Name, Jesus, Amen. **Romans 10:9-10**

DAY 3

Prayer to Remove
Reproach and Contempt

Psalm 119:17-24
GIMEL
(Pronounced "geeh-mel")

Deal bountifully with Your servant,
That I may live and keep Your Word.
Open my eyes,
That I may see wondrous things from Your law.
I am a stranger in the earth;
Do not hide Your commandments from me.
My soul breaks with longing for
Your judgments at all times.
You rebuke the proud - the cursed,
Who stray from Your commandments.
Remove from me reproach and contempt,
For I have kept Your testimonies.
Princes also sit and speak against me,
But Your servant **meditates** on Your statutes.
Your testimonies also are my delight and my counselors.

11

The Beer Bottle

When I was a freshman in high school there was a girl at the school I attended that didn't like me, and wanted to beat me up. I couldn't understand why, I didn't know her; I had just moved to the area and didn't know anyone. In my fear, I asked my uncle (a modern day outlaw) "What do I do?" His response was: "Pick up a beer bottle, she won't touch you"…well, that wasn't the case. I did pick up a bottle as she came at me. In response to being slugged in the face, I hit her in the head. When the police arrived, I explained to them that she hit me first, and I was defending myself. She was taken to the hospital; I was taken to juvenile hall. She suffered a concussion; I was isolated for three days.

After three days I was released to house arrest with an ankle bracelet and a court date. The other girl was released from the hospital the following day and was ok. Thank You, Lord Jesus!

When I went to court, I was charged with assault with a deadly weapon. But because I had no previous history of this type of crime, I was given 3 years of probation. In one year I was released from my probation, and this offense is nowhere to be found in my history. God removed this reproach and the contempt that could have followed me!

As I reflect back on my life before I surrendered to the Lordship of Jesus Christ. I see that His grace was there. It is so amazing for me to think that while I was yet a sinner, he died for me, to wash me clean, purging me of all my sin and shame.

Supporting Scriptures

Psalm 116:7 Return to your rest, O my soul, for the Lord has dealt bountifully with you.

Psalm 39:12 Hear my prayer, O, Lord, and give ear to my cry; Do not be silent at my tears; for I am a stranger with You, a sojourner, as all my fathers were.

Hebrews 11:13 These all died in faith, not having received the promises, but having seen them afar off were assured of them, embraced them and confessed that they were strangers and pilgrims on the earth.

Psalm 42:1-2 As the deer pants for the water brooks, so my soul pants for You, O God. My soul thirsts for God, for the living God. When shall I come and appear before God?

Psalm 63:1 O God, You are my God; Early will I seek You; My soul thirsts for You; My flesh longs for You. In a dry and thirsty land where there is no water.

Psalm 84:2 My soul longs, yes, even faints for the courts of the Lord; My heart and my flesh cry out for the living God.

Psalm 39:8 Deliver me from all my transgressions; Do not make me the reproach of the foolish.

Key Word Definition

Reproach:
1) Censure (censure means: the act of blaming or finding fault) mingled with contempt or derision; contumelious or opprobrious language towards any person; s abusive reflections; as foul-mouthed reproach.

13

2) Shame; infamy; disgrace. (Give not thine heritage to reproach. Joel 2, Isaiah 5)

3) Object of contempt, scorn or derision. (Come, and let us build up the wall of Jerusalem, that we may be no more a reproach. Nehemiah 2)

4) That which is the cause of shame or disgrace. (Genesis 30)

Strong's Concordance: H2781 kher-paw' From H2778: contumely, disgrace, the pudenda; - rebuke, reproach (-fully), shame.

Total KJV Occurrences 73

Contempt:
1) The act of despising: the act of viewing or considering and treating as mean, vile and worthless; disdain; hatred of what is mean or deemed vile. This word is one of the strongest expressions of a mean opinion which the language affords.

2) The state of being despised; whence in a scriptural sense, shame, disgrace. (Some shall awake to everlasting contempt. Daniel 12)

3) In law, disobedience of the rules and orders of a court, which is a punishable offense.

Strong's Concordance: H937 booz From H936; disrespect: - contempt (-uously), despised, shamed.

Total KJV Occurrences: 11

14

Time of Reflection

Are there places in my life that need to change? List them out, and write a plan as to what that would look like.

_____

_____

_____

_____

_____

_____

_____

_____

_____

_____

_____

Prayer for Deliverance

Father, I ask that You forgive me for all pride, arrogance, and rebellion. That You would deliver me of everything that does not please You. There is no good thing in my flesh! I pray for Your healing and deliverance. Remove every wicked place from my heart. The enemy of my soul would seek to destroy me from the inside out. I ask that You give me a clean heart, that You would wash my mind from memories that would torment me and give me peace. This day I choose to love You with my whole heart. In Jesus Name, Amen. **Psalm 51:10**

DAY 4

Revive Me According To Your Word

Psalm 119:25-32
DALETH
(Pronounced "da'leth")

My soul clings to the dust;
Revive me according to Your Word.
I have declared my ways, and You answered me;
Teach me Your statutes.
Make me understand the way of Your precepts;
So shall I **meditate** on Your wonderful works.
My soul melts from heaviness;
Strengthen me according to Your Word.
Remove from me the way of lying,
And grant me Your law graciously.
I have chosen the way of Truth;
Your judgments I have laid before me.
I cling to Your testimonies;
O Lord, do not put me to shame!
I will run the course of Your commandments,
For You shall enlarge my heart.

An Unruly Teenager

I was an unruly teenager. My parents divorced when I was 4 years of age, and at the age of 7, my sister and I went to live with our father. I don't have a lot of memories of my life prior to that, only that of walking home from school unattended and being alone watching my little sister.

When I was young, I never understood where my mom went until I was older. You see my mom was only 15 when she became pregnant with me; she became a mother at the age of 16. I found out much later in life that she decided to run away and join the carnival, and travel from city to city and state to state. My thought was that deep down inside she was trying to find something that was lost.

I had a sincere desire to go back to live with her, and when I was 12, I was told, that if you call your aunt she will come to pick you up, and you can live with your mom. So one day I did just that, I ran away from my dad and my little sister, to go live with my mom.

From that time forward I decided that if I wanted a change, all I needed to do was run away. I became a runner, don't want to stay in class, I would ditch. Don't like the rules at home, I would leave, and stay out all night. Don't like the job, I would quit.

I started some terrible habits in my life. I dropped out of high school, started doing drugs, drinking uncontrollably and always running away from my problems. And this continued until I surrendered to the Lord Jesus Christ on June 2, 1986.

Supporting Scriptures

Psalm 143:11-12 Revive me, O Lord, for Your Name's sake! For Your righteousness' sake bring my soul out of trouble. In Your mercy cut off my enemies and destroy all those who afflict my soul; for I am Your servant.

Psalm 25:4-5 Show me Your ways, O Lord; teach me Your paths, lead me in Your Truth and teach me, for You are the God of my salvation; On You I wait all the day. (Psalm 27:11, Psalm 86:11)

*Psalm 145:5-6 I will **meditate** on the glorious splendor of Your majesty, and on Your wondrous works. Men shall speak of the might of Your awesome acts, and I will declare Your greatness.*

1 Kings 4:29 And God gave Solomon wisdom and exceedingly great understanding, and largeness of heart, like the sand on the seashore.

Isaiah 60:5 Then you shall see and become radiant, and your heart shall swell with joy; because of the abundance of the sea shall be turned to you, the wealth of the Gentiles shall come to you.

2 Corinthians 6:11-14 O Corinthians! We have spoken openly to you, our heart is wide open, you are not restricted by us, but you are restricted by your own affections. Now in return for the same (I speak as to children), you also be open. Do not be unequally yoked together with unbelievers. For what fellowship has righteousness with lawlessness? And what accord has Christ with Belial? Or what part has a believer with an unbeliever?

18

Key Word Definition

Revive:
1) To bring again to life; to reanimate.

2) To raise from languor, (…) depression or discouragement; to rouse; as, to revive the spirits or courage.

3) To renew; to bring into action after a suspension; as, to revive a project or scheme that had been laid aside.

4) To renew in the mind or memory; to recall.
    The mind has the power in many cases to revive ideas or perceptions, which it has once had.
        Locke.

5) To recover from a state of neglect or depression; as, to revive letters or learning.

6) To re-comfort; to quicken; to refresh with joy or hope.

7) To bring again into notice.

Strong's Concordance: H2421 (definition for **quicken**; NKJV changed to revive) khaw-yaw' A prim root (compare H2331, H2424); to live, whether literally or figuratively; causatively to **revive**; - keep (leave, make) alive, X certainly, give (promise) life, (let, suffer to) live, nourish up, preserve (alive), quicken, recover, repair, restore (to life), revive, (X God) save (alive, life, lives), X surely, be whole.

Total KJV Occurrences: 26

Time of Reflection

Is there a place in my life that needs to be revived and brought back to Life?

_____

_____

_____

_____

_____

_____

_____

_____

_____

_____

_____

Prayer for Change

    Father, I ask You to heal my mind in such a way, that You give me the ability to think differently. I ask that You change my mind and help me to think the thoughts that You have for me. I ask that You remove from me all lying and every form of deception. Whether I have deceived or have been deceived. I ask You with my whole heart to remove it far from me! I thank You that the thoughts that You have for me are to give me a hope and a future. Please let me see it, In the mighty Name of Jesus! Amen. **Jeremiah 29:11**

DAY 5

Revive Me
In Your Way

Psalm 119:33-40
HEH
(Pronounced HEH)

Teach me, O Lord, the way of Your **statutes**,
And I shall keep it to the end.
Give me understanding, and I shall keep Your law;
Indeed, I shall observe it with my whole heart.
Make me walk in the path of Your commandments,
For I delight in it.
Incline my heart to Your testimonies,
And not to covetousness.
Turn away my eyes from looking at worthless things,
And revive me in Your way.
Establish Your Word to Your servant,
Who is devoted to fearing You.
Turn away my reproach, which I dread,
For Your judgments are good.
Behold, I long for Your **precepts;**
Revive me in Your righteousness.

21

Influenced By Others

Learning to live a surrendered life didn't come easy! You see, I was taught to run away when you want things to change. I had created bad habits of escaping out of situations when I didn't get my way. I started experimenting with drugs at the age of 12. When I was 14, I started drinking alcohol, which then led down the path of sexual promiscuity.

When I was 16, I became pregnant. I thought I was ready for motherhood, my boyfriend and I chose to move in with my father. Then one day, my boyfriend was offered a job out of town and left me alone at my father's home in the High Desert of California. I felt abandoned (again), alone, and not knowing what to do, so I called my mom in Bakersfield and went back to live with her.

We were influenced by so many voices being told "You are too young," "How are you going to take care of your child?" "You can't take care of yourselves, how are you going to take care of a baby?" Within 2 weeks my boyfriend and I had made the decision to abort our baby. I still remember the day so well. I was torn, with wanting my baby, but being influenced that this was the best thing for my life, being so young.

I didn't have any idea of what that decision would do to me for many years to come. It became a living torment that would never stop. The alcohol could not remove the pain and void that I had. I had a horrible hole in my heart that could never be filled. I became filled with anger, fear, rejection, abandonment, insecurity, and so much more. I started blaming others for the decision that I had made.

Three years later I was faced with being pregnant again. I couldn't believe it! You think I would have learned by now. But the one thing that was different about this time was, that even though I was still young, I knew that I wanted to keep my baby. My boyfriend at the time tells me…"If you abort this child, we can still be friends." I knew without a shadow of a doubt that I didn't need a friend like that. I chose to keep my baby and to birth him without his biological father in our lives. I can't say that having a baby without the support of a father is the way to go. But I knew I could not add to the torment that I was already living in.

I became a single mother at the age of nineteen and had a perfectly healthy baby boy, 8 pounds 5 ounces, 21 inches long. My son's biological father's mother helped me financially to pay the hospital bill. (But said, "Please don't tell anyone") I found out that I wasn't the only one carrying the shame of the decisions I had made.

I was very thankful for the support of my family during this time, aunts and uncles gave me the encouragement to keep going, and to make the needed changes of not giving up. My aunt Connie let me live with them while I was pregnant, and told me "Tonja, everyone thinks you are going to fail, prove them wrong!" (Thank you, Aunt Connie!!) I think it must have been the Irish in me, maybe the German, but that day, I set a course to do just that, prove them wrong. I soon found out, I could not do this without the help of the Lord Jesus Christ.

Supporting Scriptures

Revelations 2:26 *And he who overcomes, and keeps My works until the end, to him I will give power over the nations.*

Proverbs 2:6 *For the Lord gives wisdom; From His mouth come knowledge and understanding;*

James 1:5 *If any of you lacks wisdom, let him ask of God, who gives to all liberally and without reproach, and it will be given to him.*

Mark 7:14-23 *When He called all the multitude to Himself, He said to them, "Hear Me, everyone, and understand: There is nothing that enters a man from outside which can defile him; but the things which come out of him, those are the things that defile a man. If anyone has ears to hear, let him hear!"*

When He had entered a house away from the crowd, his disciples asked him concerning the parable. So He said, ***"What comes out of a man, that defiles a man. For from within, out of the heart of men, proceed evil thoughts, adulteries, fornications, murders, thefts, covetousness, wickedness, deceit, lewdness, an evil eye, blasphemy, pride, foolishness. All these evil things come from within and defile a man."***

Luke 12:15 *And He said to them, take heed and beware of covetousness, for one's life does not consist in the abundance of the things he possesses."*

Hebrews 13:5 *Let your conduct be without covetousness; be content with such things as you have.*

Key Word Definition

Establish:

1) To set and fix firmly or unalterably: to settle permanently.
I will *establish* my covenant with him for an everlasting covenant. Genesis 17

2) To found permanently; to erect and fix or settle; as to establish a colony or an empire.

3) To enact or decree by authority and for permanence; to ordain; to appoint; as, to establish laws, regulations, institutions, rule, ordinances.

4) To settle or fix; to confirm; as, to establish a person, society or corporation, in possessions or privileges.

5) To make firm; to confirm; to ratify what has been previously set or made.
Do we then make void the law through faith? God forbid: yea, we *establish* the law. Romans 3

Strong's Concordance: Stablish H5650 *koom* A primitive root; to rise (in various applications, literally, figuratively, intensively and causatively); - abide, accomplish, X be clearer, confirm, continue, decree, X be dim, endure, X enemy, enjoin, get up, make good, help, hold, (help to) lift up (again), make, X but newly, ordain, perform, pitch, raise (up), rear (up), remain, (a-) rise (up) (again, against), rouse up, set (up), stir up, strengthen, succeed, (as-, make) sure (-ly), (be) up (-hold, -rising).

Total KJV Occurrences: 628

Time of Reflection

Were there times in my life that I was influenced by others to make decisions in my life?

_____

_____

_____

_____

_____

_____

_____

_____

_____

_____

_____

Prayer of Commitment

Father, today, I choose to take responsibility for the decisions that I have made in my life, and even though as a child I may have been influenced by others, this day I thank You for forgiving me for ALL of my sins. Now, I ask for the ability to make the right decisions based on You leading me and delivering me from every form of fear. I thank You that You have not given me the spirit of fear, but of power, love, and a sound mind. This day, I choose to follow Your voice, and not the voice of anyone else!! In Jesus Name, I pray, Amen. **2 Timothy 1:7**

DAY 6

I Trust
In Your Word

Psalm 119:41-48
MEV(WAW)
(Pronounced VAHV)

Let Your mercies come to me, O Lord
Even Your deliverance according to Your Word.
So shall I have an answer for him who reproaches me,
For I trust in Your Word.
Do not take the Word of Truth out of my mouth,
For I have hoped in Your judgments.
So shall I keep Your law continually, forever and ever.
And I will walk in an open space,
For I seek Your precepts.
I will speak of Your testimonies also before kings,
And will not be ashamed.
I will delight myself in Your commandments,
Which I have loved.
My hands I will lift up to Your commandments,
Which I have loved;
I will **meditate** on Your statutes.

Supernatural Healing

It was the mid 90's, and my husband had taken a ministry trip while I stayed home with our children. All of a sudden I became overwhelmed with emotion. My thoughts were irrational, and I was very irritable. I couldn't seem to control my emotions; I felt abandoned, rejected, and completely alone. Irrepressible anger, bitterness, and resentment were widespread in my life in the early years of my marriage. So much, in fact, that I was unable to function when this anger would be aroused. I would fight depression horribly.

When my husband returned, he took the time to pray with me; all of a sudden a well of uncontrollable sobbing tears arose from deep within my being. I couldn't stop crying. As my husband prayed for me, he held me as a father would hold his little girl. He asked our heavenly Father to reveal the root cause of my deep pain. In a flash, the Lord opened my spiritual eyes and gave me a vision of heaven. I suddenly saw a little girl with blue eyes and blond hair, she looked like my mother, and my grandfather was holding her. I immediately knew that this was my baby girl, the one I had aborted. I asked the Lord to please forgive me, again. You see, often times I would repent for this sin over and over, but never felt the forgiveness or shame lift. But this moment was unlike any of the others. Immediately, I felt the Lord's forgiveness, healing, and unconditional love. He washed me of this horrible pain and shame. Seeing my little girl in the arms of my grandfather at the throne of God brought such healing to me. I saw joy and peace on my little girl as my grandfather held her in his arms. It removed the sorrow that had been bottled up within me for over 15 years!

The Lord not only healed me of the pain that was engulfed in my shame. But He set me free of the depression that bound me. I was able to forgive myself, as well as others. I repented of un-forgiveness, starting with myself. As I did this, the Lord began to show me the places of bitterness and resentment that I held so tightly, which I was now able to release. The Lord showed me that the cycle of these three together, un-forgiveness, bitterness, and resentment are what created the dysfunction in my life. These three lies disabled me and kept me from being able to function normally. I would literally not be able to get out of my bed, or off the couch. I was in complete DYSFUNCTION.

Since that day, I have had the opportunity to share this testimony with hundreds of women, and pray for numerous ones to be healed of this same type of pain. Each time I prayed, I had the amazing pleasure to see our heavenly Father touch each one uniquely, and restore the deep places of their heart. In Revelations 12:11 it says "And they overcame him by the blood of the Lamb and the word of their testimony;"

Supporting Scriptures

Proverbs 4:10-13 *Hear, my son, and receive my sayings, and the years of your life will be many. I have taught you in the way of wisdom; I have led you in right paths. When you walk, your steps will not be hindered, and when you run, you will not stumble. Take firm hold of instruction, do not let go; Keep her for she is your life.*

Matthew 10:16-20 *Behold, I send you out as sheep in the midst of wolves. Therefore be wise as serpents and harmless as doves. But beware of men, for they will deliver you up to councils and scourge you in their synagogues. You will be brought before governors and kings for My sake, as a testimony to them and to the Gentiles. But when they deliver you up, do not worry about how or what you should speak. For it will be given to you in that hour what you should speak; for it is not you who speaks, but the Spirit of your Father who speaks in you.*

Key Word Definitions

Trust: Confidence; a reliance or resting of the mind on the integrity, veracity, justice, friendship or other sound principle of another person. (He that put his trust in the Lord shall be safe. Proverbs 29)

Strong's Concordance: H982 baw-takh' A primitive root; properly to hide for refuge (but not so precipitately as H2620); figuratively to trust, be confident or sure: - be bold (confident, secure, sure). Careless (one, woman), put confidence, (make to) hope, (put, make to) trust.

30

Total KJV occurrences: 120

Time of Reflection

Are there people that have been in my life that I need to forgive? (Including yourself)

_____
_____
_____
_____
_____
_____
_____
_____
_____
_____
_____

Could there be a place of bitterness, or resentment that resends information over and over in your mind that needs to be cut out and repented of? *(If you want to break a habit in your life, you must change and do things different!)*

_____
_____
_____
_____
_____
_____
_____
_____
_____
_____
_____

Prayer of Trust

Father, this day I choose to forgive others and myself. I choose to trust You! I have decided to follow Your voice and not the voice of a stranger. Help me to know who You are. Cause me to see with Your eyes, with Your heart, and to love, forgive, and to live my life in the freedom that You have given me. I love You, Jesus! I ask that You make me sensitive to Your Holy Spirit's gentle nudging and that You would lead and guide me every step of the way. In Jesus Name I pray, Amen. **1 John 1:9**

DAY 7

Your Word
Has Given Me Life

Psalm 119:49-56
ZAYIN
(Pronounced ZAH-yeen)

Remember Your Word to Your servant,
In which You have made me hope.
This is my comfort in my affliction.
That Your Promise gives me life.
The insolent utterly deride me,
But I do not turn away from Your law.
When I think of Your rules from of old,
I take comfort, O Lord.
Hot indignation seizes me because of the wicked,
Who forsake Your law.
Your statutes have been my songs;
In the house of sojourning.
I remember Your Name in the night, O Lord,
And keep Your law.
This blessing has fallen to me,
That I have kept Your precepts. (ESV)

33

I've Never Walked Alone

As I grew in my faith, I learned to soak (worship) in the Presence of the Lord. I would get up every morning, and meet with Him in my living room. I had created a spiritual altar right in front of our television (it stayed off most of the time). Some days I would be there for hours. My friends would come over, and we would soak and pray. My daughters would come downstairs and soak and pray. We created a spiritual pool right in the center of our living room. God's Presence would bring healing, life, and joy. When we would have prayer meetings, the Lord would answer without delay. We encountered many times, with immediate answers to prayer, and amazing visitations.

After several years of this going on, my husband was starting to get a little frustrated with me. Not about the praying, but that the housework was not getting accomplished to his liking. Dishes were piling up, laundry was overflowing - our home was completely out of order. So I did my best to start changing, with prayer/soaking less and accomplishing my housework; laundry, cooking, and dishes more.

A few weeks later, while I was doing my dishes and looking out my kitchen window, the Lord spoke to me loud and clear, "Tonja, you can't live here, but I want you to stay." My response was, "Ok Lord," but in reality, I had no comprehension of what He said. I pondered it in my heart for weeks, even months, repeating it over and over in my mind; I was heartbroken, did He want me to leave Him and His Presence? This was the last thing I ever wanted to do!

Then one day, I got it. He was telling me that I can't live on my face every day, but as I go about my household chores and responsibilities that I could stay in His Presence continually. That day was very liberating for me! The revelation and understanding that I could stay in God's Presence every moment of every day was like taking a breath of fresh air of incredible liberation!

The freedom of staying in His Presence wherever I went caused me to jump into the next season of my life. I now knew that I could access Him wherever I am, and wherever I go, just like a best friend who never leaves me nor forsakes me.

He has taught me that even though I walk through the valleys, and even some very difficult places, I have never walked alone. He is always with me wherever I go.

Supporting Scriptures

Romans 15:4-6 *For whatever things were written before were written for our learning, that we through the patience and comfort of the Scriptures might have hope. Now may the God of patience and comfort grant you to be like-minded toward one another, according to Christ Jesus, that you may with one mind and one mouth glorify the God and Father of our Lord Jesus Christ.*

Psalm 63 *O God, You are my God; Early will I seek You; My soul thirsts for You; My flesh longs for You in a dry and thirsty land where there is no water. So I have looked for You in the sanctuary, to see Your power and Your glory.*

Because Your loving-kindness is better than life, my lips shall praise You. Thus, I will bless You while I live; I will lift up my hands in Your Name. My soul shall be satisfied as with marrow and fatness, and my mouth shall praise You with joyful lips.

When I remember You on my bed, I meditate on You in the night watches. Because You have been my help, therefore in the shadow of Your wings I will rejoice. My soul follows close behind You; Your right hand upholds me.

But those who seek my life, to destroy it, shall go into the lower parts of the earth. They shall fall by the sword; They shall be a portion for jackals.

But the king shall rejoice in God; everyone who swears by Him shall glory; But the mouth of those who speak lies shall be stopped.

Key Word Definition

Life: The present state of existence; the time from birth to death. The life of man seldom exceeds seventy years.

If in this life only we have hope in Christ, we are of all men most miserable. 1 Corinthians 15

Strong's Concordance: Life translated from "quickened" H2421 Khaw-yaw' a prim root (compare H2331, H2424): to live, whether literally or figuratively; causatively to revive; -keep (leave, make) alive, X certainly, give (promise) life, (let, suffer to) live, nourish up, preserve (alive), quicken, recover, repair, restore (to life), revive, (X God) save (alive, life, lives:, X surely, be whole.

Total KJV Occurrences: 264

37

Time of Reflection

What is my daily devotional time like?

Write out some ways that you can live a life of Worship

_____

_____

_____

_____

_____

_____

_____

_____

_____

_____

_____

Prayer for the Day

Father, I ask that You let my life be pleasing in everything I would do and say. I pray today and ask that You would put a guard in my mouth so that I would not sin against You. I ask that You lead me in the fullness of who You are.

I put on the **full armor of God** standing with my **waist girded with Truth**, putting on the **breastplate of righteousness**, and having **shod my feet with peace**. I take up the **shield of faith** so that I can quench every fiery dart of the enemy. And I put on the **helmet of salvation**, and I take up the **Sword of the Spirit**, which is the Word of God.

Help me to be watchful in the midst of a perverse generation! **Ephesians 6:10-18**

DAY 8

The Lord Is My Portion

Psalm 119:57-64
KHET
(Pronounced KHEHT)

The Lord is my portion;
I promise to keep Your Words.
I entreat Your favor with all my heart;
Be gracious to me according to your promise.
When I think on my ways,
I turn my feet to Your testimonies.
I hasten, and do not delay
To keep Your commandments.
Though the cords of the wicked ensnare me,
I do not forget Your law.
At midnight I rise to praise You,
Because of Your righteous rules.
I am a companion of all who fear You,
Of those who keep Your precepts.
The earth, O Lord, is full of Your steadfast love;
Teach me Your statutes! (ESV)

I Barely Made It

It was 1995; I was still asleep but slowly waking. As I was waking up, I started seeing myself walking down a long dirt road. As I looked at myself, my clothes were torn from head to toe. I was bloody as if beaten and was trying to walk straight ahead, but with all my strength, I was barely making it. Suddenly I looked up and saw an old rugged door surrounded by overgrown Ivy, so much, in fact, I was almost unable to see its door handle. As soon as I recognized the door, I was given a new strength to get to the handle, but before I touched it, it opened. I saw a glorious light shining; it was the Lord, my precious Jesus. He looked at me and immediately gave me a fresh new gown of pure white. Instantly I was clean, and all the pain was gone.

When I awoke from what I thought to be a dream, but later realizing it was a vision. I pondered what I saw and the one thing that I kept processing even to this day is: I was barely making it to the door. "I BARELY MADE IT!"

I started digging into the scriptures trying to find something to confirm this vision, and I found Mathew 7:14 Because the gate is straight, and the way *difficult* that leadeth unto life, and few there be that find it. I then realized that being a Christian was more than just reading the bible to my children, and going to services twice a week. I came to find out, that it was learning to be forgiving when those closest to you, betray you. I learned that I couldn't let the actions of others keep me from becoming like Jesus.

It is now 2018, and I have experienced many difficulties in my life, and I've had millions of opportunities to forgive, and forgive again. Learning to live a surrendered life hasn't been easy; in fact, it has been a painful one. I keep reminding myself to keep my focus on the Lord. To keep my eyes lifted up and upon Him. Knowing that HE will bring me through every circumstance, and every pain. Every pain was washed away when I BEHELD HIM.

Supporting Scriptures

Numbers 18:20 Then the Lord said to Aaron; You shall have no inheritance in their land, nor shall you have any portion among them; I am your portion and your inheritance among the children of Israel.

Psalm 16:5-11 O Lord, You are the portion of my inheritance and my cup; You maintain my lot. The lines have fallen to me in pleasant places; Yes, I have a good inheritance. I will bless the Lord who has given me counsel; My heart also instructs me in the night seasons. I have set the Lord always before me; Because He is at my right hand I shall not be moved. Therefore my heart is glad, and my glory rejoices; My flesh also will rest in hope. For You will not leave my soul in Sheol, Nor will You allow Your Holy One to see corruption. You will show me the path of life; In Your presence is fullness of joy; At Your right hand are pleasures forevermore.

Jeremiah 10:6 There is none like You O Lord, You are great, and Your Name is great in might.

Lamentations 3:22-26 Through the Lord's mercies we are not consumed, because His compassions fail not. They are new every morning; Great is Your faithfulness. "The Lord is my portion," says my soul; "Therefore I hope in Him!" The Lord is good to those who wait for Him, to the soul who seeks Him. It is good that one should hope and wait quietly for the salvation of the Lord.

Luke 15:17-18 But when he came to himself, he said, How many of my father's hired servants have bread enough and to spare, and I perish with hunger! I will arise and go to my father, and will say to him "Father, I have sinned against heaven and before you.

Acts 16:25-26 But at midnight Paul and Silas were praying and singing hymns to God, and the prisoners were listening to them. And suddenly there was a great earthquake, so that the foundation of the prison was shaken; and by and by all the doors opened, and every man's bands were loosed.

Psalm 33:4-5 For the Word of the Lord is right, and all His work is done in Truth. He loves righteousness and justice; The earth is full of the goodness of the Lord.

Key Word Definition

Portion: A part of a whole; an amount, section, or a piece of something.

The priests had a portion assigned to them of Pharaoh. Genesis 47

Strong's Concordance: H2506 khay'-lek From H2505; properly smoothness (of the tongue): also an *allotment*: - flattery, inheritance, part, X partake, portion.

Total KJV Occurrences: 67

43

Time of Reflection

Identify the Lord's goodness in your life. Write out the blessings that you have received.

_____

_____

_____

_____

_____

_____

_____

_____

_____

_____

_____

Prayer of Faith

Father, I ask for Faith today. That Faith, to speak to the mountains in my life to be removed! And when I walk through difficult places, I choose to find comfort in You, the Author and the Finisher of My faith! I will not fear what man can do to me, because I know that You are with me. I ask that You give me an understanding of Your Word, let me see and feel You in the midst of the storms of life. I thank You that you said You would never leave me nor forsake me. I thank You that You are my very present help, and You give me the strength to overcome every obstacle. **Psalm 23**

DAY 9

I Will Keep Your Precepts With My Whole Heart

Psalm 119:65-72
TET
(Pronounced TEHT)

You have dealt well with Your servant,
O Lord, according to Your Word.
Teach me good judgment and knowledge,
For I believe Your commandments.
Before I was afflicted I went astray,
But now I keep Your Word.
You are good, and do good;
Teach me Your statutes.
The proud have forged a lie against me,
But I will keep Your precepts with my whole heart.
Their heart is as fat as grease,
but I delight in Your law.
It is good for me that I have been afflicted,
That I may learn Your statutes.
The law of Your mouth is better to me
Than thousands of coins of gold and silver.

I Wasn't Like Most Girls

I had just pulled up to my babysitter's apartment, Ken had been working at a new construction sight across the street, and walked over from the job sight when he saw me arrive. I hadn't even gotten out of the car yet, and he opened my door, kneeled down on one knee, and asked me to be his wife. The first feeling was total fear as my emotions ran through my body all at once! The second was complete confusion, then an overwhelming sense of being dumbfounded! Yes, dumbfounded, I felt like a mute, and couldn't speak. I wanted to say yes, but I was afraid, I wanted to speak, but I didn't know how to communicate all of the emotions that I felt. It was like I was going to uncork and explode all over the parking lot. I knew I needed to respond, so I asked him if could tell him the following day?

Well, tomorrow came, and I needed to give Ken an answer. I still didn't know how to respond. I chose to say "No." To this day I am not quite sure how it came out of my mouth, but that fear had overtaken me in such a way, I couldn't imagine how I could be his wife. You see, my parents divorced when I was 4, and both of them remarried 3 times. I didn't want to get married, only to divorce. So I knew that it would be for LIFE when I chose to say, "I DO."

Most girls start dreaming of their wedding day, planning it, designing their dress, but I wasn't like most girls. I had no idea what that type of dream was. I had never imagined myself being a wife. So when Ken proposed to me, it opened an entirely different world of something I didn't even comprehend. You see, through my entire life I bounced around from house to house, aunts and uncles, grandma and grandpas, and then as I became a teenager, it was wherever

I landed. So the security of a husband, family, and a home of my own wasn't even a category I could comprehend.

All I could remember from that day was the great disappointment that Ken went through, his response was; "Well then, if you are not going to be my wife, then we can't be around each other." Ken had been my Single's Pastor, he had prayed for me to be filled with the Holy Spirit, and I was set free from drugs supernaturally overnight! He had been teaching me the ways of the Lord, and now all of a sudden, "If you are not going to be my wife, we can't be seen together." I felt like I lost my best friend. I went for several months, still attending bible studies, but he was keeping his distance.

Then one day, he realized I was missing him, and told me, that if you are going to be my wife, then you are going to have to ask me to marry you. Yes, the day came and I had to ask him if he would still accept me to be his wife. He said yes. I found out later that he wanted to say no. I think because of pride and him being butthurt…but he didn't.

We lived happily ever after….NOT….without trials.

Supporting Scriptures

Philippians 1:9-11 *This I pray, that your love may abound more and more in knowledge and all discernment, that you may approve the things that are excellent, that you may be sincere and without offense till the day of Christ, being filled with the fruits of righteousness which are by Jesus Christ, to the glory and praise of God.*

Proverbs 3:11 *My son do not despise the chastening of the Lord, nor detest His correction.*

Hebrews12:5-12 *And you have forgotten the exhortation addressed to you as sons:*

"My son, do not despise the discipline from the Lord, nor grow weary when you are rebuked by Him; for whom the Lord loves He disciplines, and scourges every son whom He receives."

Endure discipline; God is dealing with you as with sons. For what son is there whom a father does not discipline? If you are without discipline, of which everyone has partaken, then you are illegitimate children and not sons. Furthermore, we have had human fathers, and they corrected us, and we gave them reverence. Shall we not much more be subject to the Father of spirits and live? For they indeed disciplined us for a short time according to their own judgment, but He does so for our profit, that we may partake of His holiness. Now no discipline seems to be joyful at the time, but grievous. Yet afterward it yields the peaceable fruit of righteousness in those who have been trained by it. Therefore lift up your tired hands, and strengthen your weak knees. Make straight paths for your feet, lest that which is lame go out of joint, but rather be healed. (MEV)

48

Psalm 106:1-3 Praise the Lord! Oh, give thanks to the Lord, for He is good! For His mercy endures forever. Who can utter the mighty acts of the Lord? Who can declare His praise? Blessed are those who keep justice, and he who does righteousness at all times!

Psalm 19:7-11 The law of the Lord is perfect, converting the soul; The testimony of the Lord is sure, making wise the simple; The statues of the Lord are right rejoicing the heart; The commandment of the Lord is pure, enlightening the eyes, the fear of the Lord is clean, enduring forever; The judgments of the Lord are true and righteous altogether. More to be desired are they than gold, yes, than much fine gold; Sweeter also than honey and the honeycomb. Moreover by them Your servant is warned, and in keeping them there is great reward.

Proverbs 8:10-21 Receive My instruction, and not silver, and knowledge rather than choice gold; For wisdom is better than rubies, and all the things one may desire cannot be compared to it. "I, Wisdom, dwell with Prudence, and find out knowledge and discretion. The Fear of the Lord is to hate evil; Pride and arrogance and the evil way and the perverse mouth I hate. Counsel is mine, and sound wisdom; I am understanding, I have strength. By Me kings reign, and princes decree justice. By Me princes rule, and nobles, even all the judges of the earth. I love those who love Me, and those who seek Me early will find me. Riches and honor are with Me, yes, enduring riches and righteousness. My fruit is better than gold, yes, than fine gold, and My revenue than choice silver. I lead in the way of righteousness, in the midst of the paths of justice, that I may cause those who love Me to inherit wealth, and I will fill their treasuries. (MEV)

Key Word Definition

Precepts: In a general sense, any commandment or order intended as an authoritative rule of action; but applied particularly to commands respecting moral conduct. The Ten Commandments are so many precepts for the regulation of our moral conduct.

Strong's Concordance: pik-kood', pik-kood' From H6485; properly appointed, that is, a mandate (of God; plural only, collectively for the Law); -commandment, precept, statute.

Total KJV Occurrences: 24

Time of Reflection

Are there things in my life that hinder me from living a life of freedom? Take time to release those hindrances to the Lord, truly releasing forgiveness to the areas that apply and let the Holy Spirit heal those places. (Don't be in a hurry)

_____

_____

_____

_____

_____

_____

_____

_____

_____

_____

_____

Prayer for Change

Father, I ask that You change my heart, my mind, and my spirit. Make me like You! I know I cannot do this in my own strength, so today I ask You for the help to do this in You, and by Your Spirit. I thank You, that there is nothing impossible or even to difficult that You and I can't face together. Lead me by Your still small Voice, that I may hear You at all times. I thank You that I will be FREE to be ALL that You created me to be! In Jesus Name, I pray, Amen. **1 Kings 19:12**

DAY 10

Your Law Is My Delight

Psalm 119: 73-87
YUD
(Pronounced yood)

Your hands have made me and fashioned me;
Give me understanding,
That I may learn Your commandments.
Those who fear You will be glad when they see me,
Because I have hoped in Your Word.
I know, O Lord, that Your judgments are right,
And that in faithfulness You have afflicted me.
Let, I pray, Your merciful kindness be for my comfort,
According to Your Word to Your servant.
Let Your tender mercies come to me, that I may live;
For Your Law is my delight.
Let the proud be ashamed.
For they treated me wrongfully with falsehood;
But I will **meditate** on Your precepts.
Let those who fear You turn to me,
Those who know Your testimonies.
Let my heart be blameless regarding Your statutes,
That I may not be ashamed.

I Am Not Abandoned

It was 1964, my mom was 15 years old and found out she was pregnant with me. I'm sure her mind was racing as she began to think of her life changing drastically. I could only imagine what she must have been going through. Back in the early "60s," it was common to be shunned and identified as an outcast. I was told that a lovely Mormon family was going to adopt me and take her in until I was to be born. When my father realized that she was carrying his child, he went to find her and convince her to be his wife, and start their family together.

My life wasn't an easy life, it didn't start off on the right foot, in fact, I followed in my parent's footsteps of premarital pregnancy, not once, but twice. I lived with the pain (before Jesus) of not choosing to keep my first baby. But for my second child, my life was forever changed. I chose to keep my son; although I didn't experience the same thing my mom did with the father of her child, wanting to father his son.

Being a single mother caused me to realize I couldn't be a good mother without God's help. I wanted to raise my son in the Fear of the Lord. I didn't want him to face the same things I did. So I chose to turn my life over to the Lordship of Jesus Christ in full surrender to his will for both of us!

I wish that my life could have been that of better choices, especially as a teenager. But the one choice I am so thankful I made, was that of giving birth to my son, Ryan. Even in the face of opposition and financial duress, the Lord kept us, and didn't abandon either one of us!

Supporting Scriptures

Job 10:8-9 *Your hands have shaped me and made me completely, yet You destroy me. Remember, I pray, that You have made me as the clay. And would You return me to dust?*
(MEV)

Psalm 139:15-16 *My frame was not hidden from You, when I was made in secret, and skillfully wrought in the lowest parts of the earth. Your eyes saw my substance, being yet unformed. And in Your book, they all were written, the days fashioned for me, When as yet there were none of them.*

Psalm 34:2-10 *My soul shall make its boast in the Lord; the humble shall hear of it and be glad. Oh, magnify the Lord with me, and let us exalt His name together. I sought the Lord, and He heard me, and delivered me from all my fears. They looked to Him and were radiant, and their faces were not ashamed. This poor man cried out, and the Lord heard him, and saved him out of all his troubles. The angel of the Lord encamps all around those who fear Him, and delivers them. Oh taste and see that the Lord is good; blessed is the man who trusts in Him! Oh, fear the Lord, you His saints! There is no want to those who fear Him. The young lions lack and suffer hunger; but those who seek the Lord shall not lack any good thing.*

Hebrews 12:9-11 *Furthermore, we have had human fathers who corrected us, and we paid them respect. Shall we not much more readily be in subjection to the Father of spirits and live? For they indeed for a few days chastened us as seemed best to them, but He for our profit, that we may be partakers of His holiness. Now no chastening seems to be joyful for the present, but painful; nevertheless, afterward it yields the peaceable fruit of righteousness to those who have been trained by it.*

Key Word Definition

Delight:
1) A high degree of pleasure, or satisfaction of mind; joy.
    His *delight* is in the law of the Lord Psalm 1:2

2) That which gives great pleasure; that which affords delight.
    I was daily his *delight*. Proverbs 8:30

Delight is a more permanent pleasure than joy, and not dependent on sudden excitement.

To have or take great pleasure, to please highly; to give or afford high satisfaction or joy; as, a beautiful landscape delights the eye.

    I *delight* in the law of God after the inward man. Romans 7

Strong's Concordance: H8191 shah-shoo'-ah From H8173; enjoyment: -delight, pleasure.

Total KJV Occurrences: 9

Time of Reflection

Find a favorite scripture from the Word of God today, and memorize it. You can do this by singing it to a song you like, writing it on a note card and going over it repetitiously. Find what works for you.

_____

_____

_____

_____

_____

_____

_____

_____

_____

_____

_____

Prayer for your Goodness

Father, today I rejoice in You! I thank You for causing me to focus on Your goodness, and in all of the things that You find delight in. Your joy is my strength! I choose to find pleasure and delight in the promises of Your Word. I will not fear, nor turn an ear towards those things that men or women do or say, which is contrary to what You say about me. I ask for Your forgiveness for every place and time that I did not believe Your Words. And I thank You that from this day forward that I will be able to see Your goodness in everything! In Jesus Name I pray, Amen. **Nehemiah 8:10**

DAY 11

God is the Strength Of My Heart

Psalm 119:81-88
KAPH
(Pronounced Kahf)

My soul faints for Your salvation,
But I hope in Your Word.
My eyes fail from searching Your Word,
Saying, "When will You comfort me?"
For I have become like a wineskin in smoke,
Yet I do not forget Your statutes.
How many are the days of Your servant?
When will You execute judgment on those
who persecute me?
The proud have dug pits for me,
Which is not according to Your law.
All Your commandments are faithful;
They persecute me wrongfully. Help me!
They almost made an end of me on earth,
But I did not forsake Your precepts.
Revive me according to Your lovingkindness,
So that I may keep the testimony of Your mouth.

The Lord's Face

It was 1998, my husband had taken a new job at a church in Santa Barbara, but things weren't going so well. Ministry wasn't what it was at our previous church. We moved only one hour south of where we previously lived in Santa Maria, but the culture was completely different.

My husband came home one day and said, "I think I need to quit my job," things aren't going so well. We prayed together, and the Lord gave him a strategy. He was to write two documents and address some areas. The first document, if received, was how he was to walk out his release from his job. The second was if it wasn't received, he was to leave immediately.

I prayed all day the day he was to be speaking to his boss. And during this particular day, I was driving to pick up our daughter Sarah at Magic Mountain. This was a little more than an hour drive. I had some worship on in the car, and as I started singing **"If I could only see Your Face, I could make it to the end."** All of a sudden I had a full-blown vision of the Lord and His Face. I could see His passion in the fire of His eyes! I encountered a peace that flooded my entire body. When I gazed into His eyes, I became consumed by the same fire that I saw in His eyes. Suddenly, the fire shifted like beams moving up and over my head. Immediately in The Spirit, I could sense myself falling prostrate before Him, and as I looked to where the rays of fire were going, it went towards those behind me, to those that were persecuting me. I felt such divine protection and knew that NO WEAPON FORMED AGAINST US WOULD PROSPER and that whatever we were going to face, that the Lord would be with us, and nothing else mattered! (2 Thessalonians 1:6-8)

As I returned home that day from picking up Sarah, my husband said to me, "I packed up my office today, what I had to say was not received." I remember the day so well; my husband was going through many emotions all at once. He said: "What are we going to do now? How are we going to survive with neither one of us having jobs?" I was able to share my vision of the Lord's Face and His All-Consuming Presence. This brought encouragement to him, knowing that the Lord would take care of us. Together, we knew the Lord was going to walk us through whatever we needed to face on the journey the Lord had for us.

2 Thessalonians 1:6-8 It is a righteous matter with God to repay with tribulation those who trouble you, and to give you who are troubled rest with us when the Lord Jesus is revealed from heaven with His mighty angels, in flaming fire taking vengeance on those who do not know God and do not obey the gospel of our Lord Jesus Christ.

Supporting Scriptures

Psalm 73:26 My flesh and my heart fail; But **God is the** **strength of my heart** *and my portion forever.*

Psalm 84:1-8 How lovely is Your dwelling place, O Lord of Hosts! My soul longs, yes, even faints for the courts of the Lord; my heart and my body cry out for the living God.

Yes, the sparrow has found a home and the swallow a nest for herself, where she may lay her young, even at Your altars, O Lord of Hosts, my King and my God. Blessed are those who dwell in Your house; they continually praise You. Selah ~ Blessed is the man whose strength is in You, in whose heart are the paths to Zion. As they pass through the Valley of Baca, they make it a spring; the early rain also covers it with pools. They go from strength to strength; every one of them appears in Zion before God.

O Lord God of Hosts, hear my prayer, and give ear, O God of Jacob. Selah ~ Behold, O God our shield, and look upon the face of Your anointed. (MEV)

Key Word Definition

Salvation:
1) The act of saving; preservation from destruction, danger or great calamity.

2) Appropriately in theology, the redemption of man from the bondage of sin and liability to eternal death, and the conferring on him everlasting happiness. This is the great salvation.

Godly sorrow worketh repentance to salvation;

60

2 Corinthians 7

3) Deliverance from enemies; Exodus 14

4) Remission of sins, or saving graces. Luke 19

5) The author of man's salvation. Psalm 27

6) A term of praise of benediction. Revelation 19.

Strong's Concordance: H8668 tesh-oo-aw" From H7768 in the sense of H3467; rescue (literally or figuratively, personal, national or spiritual): - deliverance, help, safety, salvation, and victory.

Total KJV Occurrences: 34

Time of Reflection

Where in my life do I need salvation (deliverance, help, safety)? Let's evaluate based on the complete definition of the word.

_____

_____

_____

_____

_____

_____

_____

_____

_____

_____

_____

_____

Strength to Release Forgiveness Seventy times Seven

Father, I ask You today that You would give me the strength that I need to do Your will. Help me to lean on You and not my own understanding. Help me Lord to forgive, even seventy times seven in one day. And when my brother or sister offends me, I ask for the wisdom to go to him or her and resolve the issue in a way that is pleasing to you. I ask for Your grace to do this in Your precious Name, Jesus, Amen. **Proverbs 3:5 and Matthew 18:21**

DAY 12

Your Faithfulness Endures To All Generations

Psalm 119:89-96
LAMED
(Pronounced LAH-mehd)

Forever, O Lord,
Your Word is settled in heaven.
Your faithfulness endures to all generations;
You established the earth, and it abides.
They continue this day according to Your ordinances,
For all are Your servants.
Unless Your law had been my **delight**,
I would then have perished in my affliction.
I will never forget Your precepts,
For by them You have given me life.
I am Yours, save me;
For I have sought Your precepts.
The wicked wait for me to destroy me,
But I will consider Your testimonies.
I have seen the consummation of all perfection,
But Your commandment is exceedingly broad.

Nowhere to Live

We left Santa Barbara, in fact, we were told: "Get out of town in 30 days." And because we were taught to submit to authority (through the religious mindset) we did just that, we packed up our family and left in 30 days. Our children were not allowed to say goodbye to their friends. People in the congregation were not allowed to say goodbye to us. They wanted to come to help us pack our home, and we were threatened not to have anything to do with, "their people."

We had our home in Santa Maria, but we had leased it out for 1 year, and we still had several months to go before our 1-year was up. We had nowhere to live! Thankfully our dear friends Bill and Linda Ward (Dad and Mom in the Spirit) allowed us to live with them until we could get back into our own home. Our children all shared one bedroom. (Thank you, Bill and Linda, for putting up with all of us!)

This transition was very painful for our family, to think, these were "Christians" treating us this way? Had it not been for our personal devotion and relationship with the Lord, we may have been shipwrecked for life.

As we pursued the Lord with what to do, He began to lead us to what He desired for us. During this time, Ken had a previous commitment to travel to Texas and speak at a small church. So we followed through with what was before us. We went and ministered, and then after the services, Ken shared what we had just encountered. Thankfully this wonderful Pastor, Pastor Benny Haun (total cowboy!) had been through something very similar. Pastor Benny was able to encourage us to, "Get free from religion." This was a new concept for us, but the pain that we were encountering was so real, we knew that we needed to embrace the freedom that he was sharing with us.

God truly blessed us on that ministry trip, and that church took up an offering and sowed over $5,000.00 into our ministry! This was able to sustain us until we were able to figure out what the Lord had for us in the next season of our lives.

Supporting Scriptures

Psalm 89:2 *For I have said, "Mercy shall be built up forever; Your faithfulness You shall establish in the very heavens."*

Isaiah 40:8 *The grass withers, the flower fades, but the Word of our God stands forever."*

Matthew 24:35 *Heaven and earth will pass away, but My Words will by no means pass away.*

1 Peter 1:22-23 *Since you have purified your souls in obeying the Truth through the Spirit in sincere love of the brethren, love one another fervently with a pure heart, having been born again, not of corruptible seed but incorruptible, through the Word of God which lives and abides forever.*

Matthew 5:17-20 *Do not think that I came to destroy the Law or the Prophets. I did not come to destroy but to fulfill. For assuredly, I say to you, till heaven and earth pass away, one jot or one tittle will by no means pass from the law till all is fulfilled. Whoever therefore breaks one of the least of these commandments, and teaches men so, shall be called least in the kingdom of heaven; but whoever does and teaches them, he shall be called great in the kingdom of heaven; For I say to you, that unless your righteousness exceeds the righteousness of the scribes and Pharisees, you will by no means enter the kingdom of heaven.*

Key Word Definition

Faithfulness: Fidelity; loyalty; firm adherence to allegiance and duty as the faithfulness of a subject; Truth; veracity; as the faithfulness of God; Strict adherence to injunctions, and to the duties of a station; as the faithfulness of servants or ministers; Strict performance of promises, vows or covenants constancy in affection; as the faithfulness of a husband or wife.

Strong's Concordance H530 em-oo-naw', em-oo-naw' Feminine of H529; literally firmness; figuratively security; moral fidelity: - faith (ful, -ly –ness, [man]), set office, stability, steady, truly, truth, verily.

Total KJV Occurrences: 49

Time of Reflection

Have there been people in authority in your life that have hurt you? Take the time to release forgiveness to them.

_____

_____

_____

_____

_____

_____

_____

_____

_____

_____

_____

Prayer for Wisdom

Father, I come to You today, asking for Your wisdom in everything I do and say. Teach me Your ways, lead me in the path that You have for me. I thank You that Your Word gives me light to reveal the way that I am to walk. Lord, help me to see it. Forgive me for not trusting You! I thank You for healing in every place that I wasn't able to see You for who You are. I release forgiveness to ALL who have hurt me or caused me to see You in a wrong light. In Jesus Name, I pray, Amen. **Psalm 119: 105 and James 1:5**

DAY 13

Your Testimonies
Are My Meditation

Psalm 119:97-104
MEM
(Pronounced MEHM)

Oh, how I love Your law!
It is my **meditation** all the day.
You, through Your commandment's make me wiser than
my enemies;
For they are ever with me,
I have more understanding than all my teachers.
For Your testimonies are my meditation.
I understand more than the ancients,
Because I keep Your precepts.
I have restrained my feet from every evil way,
That I may keep Your Word.
I have not departed from Your judgments,
For You Yourself have taught me.
How sweet are Your Words to my taste,
Sweeter than honey to my mouth!
Through Your precepts, I get understanding.
Therefore I hate every false way.

69

The Nations Lord!

Upon returning to Santa Maria, we received a phone call from our Pastor. He asked Ken if we could have a meeting. He then communicated that our previous Pastor from Santa Barbara would like to bring some resolve to things that happened while you were in, "his church." Ken agreed that we would meet with him.

The day of our appointment to meet with our current Pastor and the Pastor from Santa Barbara was very unusual. Another brother was brought into the meeting with us, and he began to bring false accusations against us. This Pastor's motives were intended to remove us from the ministry completely. Under the mediation of our current Pastor, he took my husband out into the hallway and said to him, "Just agree with him, and apologize," which my husband graciously submitted to and we went on our way.

Immediately following this meeting, we headed out of town to a prayer meeting in Barstow for the weekend. As we entered into worship, a prophet identified that he saw arrows in our backs. This man had no knowledge of where we had just come from, or what we had been going through. He then said I see the spirit of Doeg chasing you, trying to kill you. The leadership prayed for us and brought an incredible refreshing portion of the Lords Spirit, healing our hearts. It was like a beautiful flow of water washing over us, healing our wounds and restoring our children.

After leaving Barstow that weekend, I started researching out Doeg because I had never heard of the spirit of Doeg before. I like to identify scriptural basis when someone starts throwing around a spirit of this, or a spirit of that. This person Doeg is found in 1 Samuel 21:7, he was an

Edomite that pursued David to kill him. In 1 Samuel 22:18 Doeg killed all the priests and their families for protecting David. This was an evil man, and he had no fear of God whatsoever.

My husband and I now realized that we were not dealing with a person, but a demonic force that wanted us cut off from any form of ministry. We submitted ourselves to the Lordship of Jesus Christ, knowing that it was He who called us, and not a man.

Shortly after this time, we found out that we were no longer licensed under our denomination because of this individual. It was heartbreaking, but we were receiving invitations to minister, so we knew that we needed to continue on ministering the gospel of Jesus Christ.

As we sought the Lord as to what to do, the Lord spoke to Ken through a vision of a birdcage, and a bird being released from its captivity…And the Lord said to him; "Do you want the nations or a denomination?" We said, "The Nations Lord!"

Since that day, my husband received a formal and public apology from the denomination, which restored his heart completely from this season of our lives. And we have been free to preach the gospel to the nations!

Supporting Scriptures

Psalm 1:1-3 *Blessed is the man who walks not in the counsel of the ungodly. Nor stands in the path of sinners, nor sits in the seat of the scornful; But his delight is in the law of the Lord, and in His law he* **meditates** *day and night. He shall be like a tree planted by the rivers of water, that brings forth its fruit in its season, whose leaf also shall not wither; and whatever he does shall prosper.*

Deuteronomy 4:5-6 *Surely I have taught you statutes and judgments, just as the Lord my God commanded me, that you should act according to them in the land which you go to posses. Therefore be careful to observe them; for this is your wisdom and your understanding in the sight of the peoples who will hear all these statutes, and say, 'Surely this great nation is a wise and understanding people.'*

2 Timothy 3:12-15 *Yes, and all who desire to live godly in Christ Jesus will suffer persecution. But evil men and impostors will grow worse and worse, deceiving and being deceived. But you must continue in the things which you have learned and been assured of, knowing from whom you have learned them, and that from childhood you have known the Holy Scriptures, which are able to make you wise for salvation through faith which is in Christ Jesus.*

Psalm 19:9-11 *The fear of the Lord is clean, enduring forever; the judgments of the Lord are true and righteous altogether. More to be desired are they than gold, yes, than much fine gold; sweeter also than honey and the honeycomb. Moreover by them Your servant is warned, and in keeping them there is great reward.*

Proverbs 8:11 *For wisdom is better than rubies, and all the things one may desire cannot be compared with her.*

Key Word Definition

Meditation: Close or continued thought; the turning or revolving of a subject in the mind; serious contemplation.

Psalm 19:14 Let the words of my mouth and the meditation of my heart be acceptable in Your sight, O LORD, my strength and my Redeemer.

Strong's Concordance: H7881 see-khaw' Feminine of H7879; *reflection*; by extension devotion: - meditation, prayer.

Total KJV Occurrences: 3

Time of Reflection

Do you know the authority that you have been given?

Take time to study Matthew 7:24-29, and 28:16-20; Write out your thoughts, and gained understanding:

_____

_____

_____

_____

_____

_____

_____

_____

_____

_____

_____

_____

Prayer to be Free from Religious Thinking

Father, I ask You to help me to follow You and not man. I know You said to submit myself to those who have authority over me. And I commit myself to live in that place of submission. Today I ask You to help me have it in its right perspective. That I would walk in the authority that You have given me, testing everything by Your Word. Give me a right spirit. Teach me to be blameless and harmless as a dove, being wise as a serpent. Make me like You! In Your precious Name, Jesus, I pray, Amen. **Matthew 10:16**

DAY 14

Your Word is a Lamp to my Feet And a Light to My Path

Psalm 119:105-112
NUN
(Pronounced NOON)

Your Word is a lamp to my feet
And a light to my path.
I have sworn and confirmed
That I will keep Your righteous judgments.
I am afflicted very much;
Revive me, O Lord, according to Your Word.
Accept, I pray, the freewill offerings of my mouth, O Lord,
And teach me Your judgments.
My life is continually in my hand,
Yet I do not forget Your law.
The wicked have laid a snare for me,
Yet I have not strayed from Your precepts.
Your testimonies I have taken as a heritage forever,
For they are the rejoicing of my heart.
I have inclined my heart to perform Your statutes
Forever to the very end.

He Wants it All

Learning to live by faith was such an incredible adventure, as the Lord was showing Himself so amazing in taking care of us. Even though we were spoken evil about, God's hand was still blessing us.

Then one day, the Lord tells my husband, "I want you to give all of your savings away into the offering." The following weekend, we were to minister in Vallejo, California at our friend's church. And the Lord gives Ken a message about destroying the Goliath's in our lives. Goliath means "debt," and God wanted to destroy the bondage of "debt" in His people's lives. That day, we were tested to give it "ALL AWAY." We now knew this was an act of obedience that was required of us. And in agreement, we did so.

That day was a monumental day in our lives. We learned that God doesn't want just a portion of us, HE WANTS IT ALL. We learned that day, that being obedient to give what God requires us to give, brings the guarantee that He will always provide for our every need and desires too.

Our heavenly Father has been so, so good to us. He has always provided extravagantly above and beyond everything we could ever ask, hope, or imagine. But, it has not come without living a life of obedience, to give what God wants, and when HE wants it. We learned that all that we have is His, and as we steward what He gives to us, by His direction that He causes us to live in a place of supernatural provision. Following His voice, and the course that He has for us in all that we do.

Supporting Scriptures

Proverbs 6:23 *The commandment is a lamp, and the law a light, reproofs of instruction are the way of life.*

Nehemiah 10:28-29 *Now the rest of the people, the priests, the Levites, the gatekeepers, the singers, the Nethinims, and all those who had separated themselves from the peoples of the lands to the Law of God, their wives, their sons, and their daughters, everyone who had knowledge and understanding; These joined with their brethren, their nobles, and entered in a curse and an oath to walk in God's Law, which was given by Moses the servant of God, and to observe and do all the commandments of the Lord our Lord, and His ordinances and His statutes;*

Hosea 14:2 *Take words with you, and return to the Lord, say to Him, take away all iniquity; Receive us graciously, for we will offer the sacrifices of our lips.*

Psalm 140:1-8 *Deliver me, O Lord, from evil men; Preserve me from violent men, who plan evil things in their hearts; They continually gather together for war. They sharpen their tongues like a serpent; The poison of asps is under their lips. Selah, Keep me, O Lord, from the hands of the wicked; Preserve me from violent men, who have purposed to make my steps stumble. The proud have hidden a snare for me, and cords; They have spread a net by the wayside; they have set traps for me. I said to the Lord; "You are my God; Hear the voice of my supplications, O Lord. O God the Lord, the strength of my salvation, You have covered my head in the day of battle. Do not grant, O Lord, the desires of the wicked; Do not further his wicked scheme, Lest they be exalted.*

Key Word Definition

Path:

1) A way beaten or trodden by the feet of man or beast, or made hard by beasts, or made hard by wheels; that part of a highway on which animals or carriages ordinarily pass.

2) Any narrow way beaten by the foot.

3) The way, course or track where a body moves in the atmosphere or in space.

4) A way or passage.

5) Course of life – He maketh all my paths. Job 33

6) Precepts; rules prescribed, uphold my goings in thy paths. Psalm 17

7) Course of providential dealings; moral government. All the paths of the Lord are mercy and truth. Psalm 25

Strong's Concordance: H5410 naw-theeb', neth-ee-baw', neth-ee-baw' From an unused root meaning to tramp; a (beaten) *track:* - [ath (way), X travel (-er), way.

Total KJV Occurrences: 26

Time of Reflection

Identify where you are obedient in giving God what He wants when He wants it?

Study Deuteronomy 28 and identify the blessings that come from obedience and the curses through disobedience. (Remember that the principles of sowing and reaping are alive and well in the New Testament)

_____
_____
_____
_____
_____
_____
_____
_____
_____
_____
_____

Prayer of Obedience

Father, I thank You that you sent your Son to show me the way to You. I thank You that Your Word is a lamp to light the "path" that You have for me! This day I choose obedience to You and not the fear of my circumstances. In the world there is uncertainty, but in You, there is hope for my future! Forgive me for every place of disobedience. Today I commit my life to the place of full surrender and obedience! I thank You for the ability to hear Your voice through Your Word, leading me every step of the way. In Jesus Name, I pray, Amen. **Jeremiah 29:11**

DAY 15

You Are My Hiding Place

Psalm 119:113-120
SAMEK
(Pronounced SAH-mehkh)

I hate the double-minded,
But I love Your law.
You are my hiding place and my shield;
I hope in Your Word.
Depart from me, you evildoers,
For I will keep the commandments of my God!
Uphold me according to Your Word,
That I may live;
And do not let me be ashamed of my hope.
Hold me up, and I shall be safe,
And I shall observe Your statutes continually.
You reject all those who stray from Your statutes,
For their deceit is falsehood.
You put away all the wicked of the earth like dross;
Therefore, I love Your testimonies.
My flesh trembles for fear of You,
And I am afraid of your judgments.

Give it All Away

Walking out into the realm of faith by giving what the Lord wanted, when He wanted it, was an amazing journey. As we would travel to churches, the Lord would speak to my husband to sow the offerings the churches would have for us. He would sow back to the church or individuals in their congregations.

After about a year of this happening, we looked back and reflected upon all of the supernatural provision, especially when God would say, "Give it all away!" So many testimonies upon returning home, there would be checks in the mail from strangers, or someone who met us three years before would tell us, "the Lord put it on our hearts to send a thousand dollars." (That would pay our house payment). **Not once were we late on our bills, not once did we go without, not once!!**

Then one day the Lord speaks to Ken and says, "I want you to quit traveling." Ken's response was; "Lord, how will I provide for my family? This is how You have been sustaining us." As Ken and I conversed, I was able to show him our financial books. And for one year, we had NOT been living on what God was bringing in through traveling, because he had been giving all of the offerings away. God had already been supernaturally providing for us. We were truly being fed like Elijah when he was in the cave, and God fed him by the ravens.

During this season in our lives, we truly learned to trust our Father in a new realm of faith. It is one thing to see it in the Word, and a completely different realm to walk it out, truly feeling His mighty right arm leading, and providing for our every need.

Supporting Scriptures

Psalm 32:7 *You are my hiding place; You shall preserve me from trouble; You shall surround me with songs of deliverance.*

Psalm 6:8 *Depart from me all you workers of iniquity; For the Lord has heard the voice of my weeping.*

Romans 5:5 *Now hope does not disappoint, because, the love of God has been poured out in our hearts by the Holy Spirit who was given to us.*

Romans 9:33 *As it is written; "Behold, I lay in Zion a stumbling stone and rock of offense, and whoever believes on Him will not be put to shame."*

Romans 10:8-11 *But what does it say? The Word is near you, in your mouth and in your heart that if you confess with your mouth the Lord Jesus and believe in your heart that God has raised Him from the dead, you will be saved. For with the heart one believes unto righteousness, and with the mouth confession is made unto salvation. For the Scripture says, "Whoever believes on Him will not be put to shame. For there is no distinction between Jew and Greek, for the same Lord over all is rich to all who call upon Him. For whoever calls on the name of the Lord shall be saved."*

Philippians 1:19-21 *For I know that this will turn out for my deliverance through your prayer and the supply of the Spirit of Jesus Christ, according to my earnest expectation and hope that in nothing I shall be ashamed, but with all boldness, as always, so now also Christ will be magnified in my body, whether by life or death. For to me, to live is Christ, and to die is gain.*

Key Word Definition

Hide (hiding): This word signified originally a station, covered place, or place of refuge for besiegers against the attacks of the besieged. Concealing; covering or withdrawing from view; keeping close or secret. **Hiding-place:** a place of concealment.

Strong's Concordance: H5643 say'-ther, sith-raw' From H5641; a cover (in a good or a bad, a literal or a figurative sense): - backbiting, covering, covert, X disguise (-th), hiding place, privily, protection, secret (-ly, place).

Total KJV Occurrences: 36

Time of Reflection

Identify the burdens in your life that you carry? Choose to cast all your cares to the Lord, and receive His peace.

_____

_____

_____

_____

_____

_____

_____

_____

_____

_____

_____

A Prayer for the Fear of the Lord

Father, I lift up every burden, and all these cares that I have been carrying and I ask for Your forgiveness for not trusting You. I release each care to You, and I lay them at Your feet. I thank You, Father, that you are my God. You are my refuge, my strong tower, and my hiding place. This day I choose to trust You in the Fear of the Lord! **Proverbs 29:25 and Isaiah 11:2**

DAY 16

I Love Your Commandments More Than Gold

Psalm 119:121-128
AYIN
(Pronounced AH-yeen)

I have done **justice** and righteousness;
Do not leave me to my oppressors.
Be surety for Your servant for good;
Do not let the proud oppress me.
My eyes fail from seeking Your salvation and Your
righteous Word.
Deal with Your servant according to Your mercy,
And teach me Your statutes.
I am Your servant; give me understanding,
That I may know Your testimonies.
It is time for You to act, O Lord,
For they have regarded Your law as void.
Therefore I love Your commandments More than gold,
Yes, than fine gold!
Therefore, all Your precepts concerning all things.
I consider to be right;
I hate every false way.

Making All Things New

It was around 9:00 PM on February 16, 2004. My husband, and our youngest 2 daughters and I were driving home from church, Southbound on the 101 Highway from Nipomo, California when a drunk driver hit our vehicle. The next thing I remember is being upside down, and my husband calling for our daughter Rachel, "Oh God, where is she, is she ok?"

Ken immediately called 911, and then started calling everyone he could think of to start praying for our family. Paramedics arrived shortly after that, and my husband was hollering at them to please go find our daughter, she isn't here. Ken and Candice were removed from the car quickly, but when it came to getting me out, they had to use the Jaws of Life. They started pulling on the door, and it was causing the safety belt to choke me. My husband then made them stop, and they were able to cut the seatbelt and then pull me out.

I was then placed into the ambulance, and they began to cut off my clothes, (my favorite leather jacket). I immediately asked the Lord, "What is going on?" I heard HIM loud and clear. He said to me "I am making all things new." I sure didn't feel new at that moment, but with those words came an overwhelming peace and comfort that surpassed the pain that my physical body had sustained.

Rachel was found a half of a football field away from our vehicle on the side of the highway, just feet away from oncoming traffic. Rachel's left leg was broken, and her spleen had been punctured, she couldn't move. Somehow an oncoming vehicle saw her on the side of the road and pulled over. Those individuals sat with Rachel and covered her until paramedics arrived. Considering how small she and it was so dark in this area of the highway, I believe this was our first miracle.

Rachel and I began physical therapy together, her for her broken leg, and me for my broken arm, neck and back. One of the first things that we were informed about regarding Rachel's broken leg was: That because she broke her leg at age14, during a time of growth, that as she would grow her broken leg would not. Rachel walked with a *slight* limp, and I struggled with this for several years. Until one day, I was at one of her water polo games, and a man with a peg leg walked by me (I think to be an angel…who has peg legs in this day and age?) And the Holy Spirit brought to my attention; she still has both her legs! To this day I am so thankful for God sparing her life. So many things could have happened to her that night.

Within a few months, my Physical Therapist informed me that he had never seen a recovery so quick as mine. I had stopped taking the pain pills 8 days after being home from the hospital (with help from my husband). And as I came back to the rightness of mind outside of the influence of the pharmaceuticals, the first thing the Lord led me to do was to release forgiveness to the drunk driver. My therapist identified my quick recovery in the absence of the pain meds. But I believe it to be the combination of the two; releasing forgiveness and receiving the healing of the Lord to help me be free from the drugs.

The recovery that I went through lasted up to 1 year of physical therapy, and several more years before I emotionally felt somewhat normal again. The one thing that I can say is that even though I walked through what felt like the darkest hour of my soul. I always knew deep inside, God was making all things new!

Supporting Scriptures

Hebrews 7:20-25 And inasmuch as He was not made priest without an oath (for they have become priests without an oath, but He with an oath by Him who said to Him: "The Lord has sworn and will not relent, You are a priest forever according to the order of Melchizedek"), by so much more Jesus has become a surety of a better covenant. Also there were many priests, because they were prevented by death from continuing. But He, because He continues forever, has an unchangeable priesthood. Therefore He is also able to save to the uttermost those who come to God through Him, since He always lives to make intercession for them.

Psalm 116:5-19 Gracious is the Lord, and righteous; Yes our God is merciful. The Lord preserves the simple; I was brought low, and He saved me. Return to your rest, O my soul, for the Lord has dealt bountifully with you. For You have delivered my soul from death, my eyes from tears, and my feet from falling. I will walk before the Lord in the land of the living. I believed, therefore I spoke, "I am greatly afflicted." I said in my haste, "All men are liars."

What shall I render to the Lord for all His benefits toward me? I will take up the cup of salvation, and call upon the name of the Lord. I will pay my vows to the Lord now in the presence of all His people.

Precious in the sight of the Lord is the death of His saints. O Lord, truly I am Your servant; I am Your servant, the son of Your maidservant; You have loosed my bonds. I will offer to You the sacrifice of thanksgiving, and will call upon the name of the Lord. I will pay my vows to the Lord now in the presence of all His people, in the courts of the Lord's house, in the midst of you, O Jerusalem. Praise the Lord!

Psalm 19:7-11 *The law of the Lord is perfect, converting the soul; The testimony of the Lord is sure, making wise the simple; The statues of the Lord are right, rejoicing the heart; The commandment of the Lord is pure, enlightening the eyes; The fear of the Lord is clean, enduring forever; The judgments of the Lord are true and righteous altogether. More to be desired are they than gold, Yea, than much fine gold; Sweeter also than honey and the honeycomb. Moreover by them Your servant is warned, and in keeping them there is great reward.*

Key Word Definition

Justice: The virtue which consists in giving to everyone what is his due; practical conformity to the laws and to principles of rectitude in the dealings of men with each other; honesty; integrity in commerce or mutual intercourse.

Strong's Concordance: H6664 tseh'-dek From H6663; the *right* (natural, moral or legal); also (abstractly) *equity* or (figuratively) *prosperity*: - X even, (X that which is altogether) just (-ice), ({un-]) right (-eous) (cause, -ly, -ness).

Total KJV Occurrences: 118

Time of Reflection

Has there been a time in your life that has hindered a healing process? Let's ask Holy Spirit to reveal any place of pain and or un-forgiveness. Go quiet, and let Him speak to you through a thought or an impression. Release forgiveness, and receive the Lord's healing in the situation.

_____

_____

_____

_____

_____

_____

_____

_____

_____

_____

Prayer to Release Forgiveness

Father, I ask You for the grace to forgive daily and to release forgiveness to those who have wronged me and to forgive myself for all areas that I've harbored within my heart. Help me to release the "What if's," The Should have's," and "Could have done things differently." Make my life a prayer to You and help me to live a life without compromise. I love You with my whole heart, help me to give it to You, entirely. In Jesus Name I pray, Amen. **Matthew 18:21-22 and Luke 17:4**

Day 17

Direct My Steps
By Your Word

Psalm 119:129-136
PE
(Pronounced PEH or PEY)

Your testimonies are wonderful;
Therefore my soul keeps them.
The entrance of Your Words gives light;
It gives understanding to the simple.
I opened my mouth and panted,
For I longed for Your commandments.
Look upon me and be merciful to me,
As Your custom is toward those who love Your Name.
Direct my steps by Your Word,
And let no iniquity have dominion over me.
Redeem me from the oppression of man,
That I may keep Your precepts.
Make Your face shine upon Your servant,
And teach me Your statutes.
Rivers of water run down from my eyes,
Because men do not keep Your law.

Keep My Focus

It was July 2004, five months after the drunk driver had detoured our lives. We had just purchased a new home and moved to Holland, Michigan. YES, all the way across the United States, while still in recovery of some significant medical issues. We had to find new doctors, new banking, a new church, a new school for our daughters, and new relationships.

As I entered our new home, I started trying to put furniture where I thought I would like it to go. I started looking for furniture that we had when we first got married, as well as furniture we didn't own. I couldn't make sense of things and was very confused. At this time, I started realizing the mental effects of the brain injury that I had experienced. It was as 10 years was erased from my memory. I knew everyone, but some memories that should have been there were just gone.

I continued to draw near to the Lord, knowing that He said, "If you draw near to Me, I will draw near to you." I was now living in a new region and what should have been an easy transition was very challenging. Learning a new address, new banking, and doctors is normally a challenge for an average person, and for me, it was doubly challenging. I was determined to not make any excuses for myself and started this journey of recovering my mind, body, and spirit.

I have found that my daddy God is so faithful, to take everything that the enemy meant for harm in my life and turn it around and use it for good! No, my recovery didn't happen overnight, but the one thing I found is: that if **"I keep my FOCUS"** on the Lord Jesus Christ, He would be faithful to get me to the other side of every difficult place.

It has now been 13 years since the drunk driver disrupted our lives. And I can tell you that time and time again, God has shown HIMSELF so faithful!

Supporting Scriptures

Proverbs 6:23 *For the commandment is a lamp, and the law a light; reproofs of instruction are the way of life.*

Psalm 19:7 *The law of the Lord is perfect, converting the soul; the testimony of the Lord is sure, making wise the simple;*

Psalm 42:1 *As the deer pants for the water brooks, so pants my soul for You, O God.*

Psalm 17:5 *Uphold my steps in Your paths, that my footsteps may not slip.*

Psalm 19:13 *Keep back Your servant from presumptuous sins; let them not have dominion over me. Then I shall be blameless, and I shall be innocent of great transgression.*

Romans 6:12-14 *Therefore do not let sin reign in your mortal body, that you should obey it in its lusts. And do not present your members as instruments of unrighteousness to sin, but present yourselves to God as being alive from the dead, and your members as instruments of righteousness to God. For sin shall not have dominion over you, for you are not under law but under grace.*

Luke 1:73-75 *The oath which He swore to our father Abraham: To grant to us that we, being delivered from the hand of our enemies, might serve Him without fear, in holiness and righteousness before Him all the days of our life.*

Numbers 6:22-27 *And the Lord spoke to Moses, saying; "Speak to Aaron and his sons, saying, 'This is the way you shall bless the children of Israel, Say to them; "The Lord* *bless you and keep you; The Lord make His face shine upon you, and be gracious to you; The Lord lift up His countenance upon you, and give you peace."'*

Psalm 4:6 *Be angry and do not sin. Meditate within your heart on your bed, and be still. Selah*

Ezekiel 9:3-4 *Now the glory of the God of Israel had gone up from the cherub, where it has been, to the threshold of the temple. And He called to the man clothed with linen, who had the writer's inkhorn at his side; and the Lord said to him, "Go through the midst of the city, through the midst of Jerusalem, and put a mark on the foreheads of the men who sigh and cry over all the abominations that are done with in it."*

Key Word Definition

In the NKJV the word "Ordered" was replaced with Direct

Ordered: Regulated; methodized; disposed; commanded; managed.

Strong's Concordance: H3358 *koon* A primitive root; properly to be *erect* (that is, stand perpendicular); Hence (causatively) to *set up*, in a great variety of applications, whether literal (*establish, fix, prepare, apply*), or figurative (*appoint, render sure, proper or prosperous*): - certain (-ty), confirm, direct faithfulness, fashion, fasten, firm, be fitted, be fixed, frame, be meet, ordain, order, perfect, (make) preparation, prepare (self), provide, make provision, (be, make) ready, right, set (aright, fast, forth), be stable, (e-) stablish, stand, tarry, X very deed.

Total KJV Occurrences: 217

Time of Reflection

Acknowledge how you are allowing the Lord to direct your steps (daily living).

_____

_____

_____

_____

_____

_____

_____

_____

_____

_____

_____

Prayer of Strength for the Journey

Father, I ask You today that You would give me the strength that I need to do Your will. Help me to lean on You and not my own understanding. In Jesus Name I pray, Amen. **Proverbs 3:5**

DAY 18

Your Law Is Truth

Psalm 119:137-144
TSADDE
(Pronounced TSAH-dee)

Righteous are You, O Lord,
And upright are Your judgments.
Your testimonies, which You have commanded,
Are righteous and very faithful.
My zeal has consumed me,
Because my enemies have forgotten Your Words.
Your Word is very pure;
Therefore, Your servant loves it.
I am small and despised,
Yet I do not forget Your precepts.
Your righteousness is an everlasting righteousness,
And Your law is Truth.
Trouble and anguish have overtaken me,
Yet Your commandments are my delights.
The righteousness of Your testimonies is everlasting;
Give me understanding and I shall live.

The Fivefold Ministry
For The Equipping of the Body of Christ

Six months after moving all the way across the United States, my husband informs me that he has been given a job opportunity back in California. He says, "Honey this is an opportunity to do what God has placed in my heart, to do church differently."

We had been serving the Lord together now for almost twenty years in ministry, and we were beginning to see the "dysfunction" in The Body of Christ. We believed God didn't intend for everyone to rely upon "The Pastor."

In 2002, The Holy Spirit had opened up the book of Ephesians to my husband in an open vision, and spoke to him about the ministry of the Apostle, Prophet, Evangelist, Pastor, and Teacher, with this Fivefold Ministry moving and working together, for the equipping of The Body of Christ to do the work of the ministry. No longer relying on "The Pastor" to do everything, but relying on one another, and CHRIST JESUS AS THE CENTER OF IT ALL.

So, we did just that! We took the job and moved back to California. Ken wrote the vision, made it plain, and began this journey of implementing the Fivefold ministry to The Body of Christ, *teaching and training* people to do the work of the ministry and giving them the confidence to rely on Holy Spirit themselves, and not a man. We identified each office gift in our church body and then released them to function in *their God-given authority*. Teaching them as Jesus did, and not as the Scribes!

Supporting Scriptures

Jeremiah 12:1 Righteous are You, O Lord, when I plead with You; yet let me talk with You about Your judgments.

Daniel 9:7 O Lord, righteousness belongs to You, but to us shame of face, as it is this day – to the men of Judah to the inhabitants of Jerusalem and all Israel, those near and those far off in all the countries to which You have driven them, because of the unfaithfulness which they have committed against You.

Daniel 9: 14 Therefore the Lord has kept the disaster in mind, and brought it upon us; for the Lord our God is righteous in all the works, which He does, though we have not obeyed His voice.

Psalm 19:7-14 The law of the Lord is perfect, converting the soul; the testimony of the Lord is sure making wise the simple; the statutes of the Lord are right, rejoicing the heart; the commandment of the Lord is pure enlightening the eyes; the fear of the Lord is clean enduring forever; the judgments of the Lord are true and righteous altogether. More to be desired are they than gold, yes, than much fine gold; sweeter also than honey and the honeycomb. Moreover by them Your servant is warned, and in keeping them there is great reward. Who can understand his errors? Cleanse me from secret faults. Keep back Your servant also from presumptuous sins; let them not have dominion over me. Then I shall be blameless, and I shall be innocent of great transgression. **Let the words of my mouth and the meditation of my heart be acceptable in Your sight, O Lord, my strength, and my Redeemer.**

Key Word Definition

Truth: Conformity to fact or reality; exact accordance with that which is, or has been, or shall be. The *truth* of history constitutes its whole value. We rely on the *truth* of the scriptural prophecies. My mouth shall speak *truth*.
Proverbs 8
Sanctify them through thy *truth*; Thy Word is *truth*.
John 17

Strong's Concordance: H571 eh'-meth Contracted from H539; stability; figuratively *certainty, truth, trustworthiness:* - assured (- ly), establishment, faithful, right, sure, true (-ly), -th), verity.

Total KJV Occurrences: 127

Time of Reflection

Are there things that I believe that are contrary to God's Word (lies about yourself or a situation)?

_____

_____

_____

_____

_____

_____

_____

Go quiet and let the Holy Spirit speak to you. Write out your thoughts, and find a scripture to counter all lies. Bring the Word (Truth) to the matter.

_____

_____

_____

_____

_____

_____

_____

_____

_____

_____

Prayer for Redemption

Thank You, Father, for Your Son Jesus, whom You sent as a ransom to save and redeem my life from destruction. I accept this gift freely, and I choose to walk in the freedom that comes with this amazing gift of salvation, where I find Your mercies are new every morning! **Matthew 20:28 Lamentations 3:22-23**

Day 19

You are Near to Those Who Draw Near to You

Psalm 119:145-152
QOPH
(Pronounced KOOF or KOHF)

I cry out with my whole heart;
Hear me, O Lord!
I will keep Your statutes.
I cry out to You;
Save me, and I will keep Your testimonies.
I rise before the dawning of the morning, and cry for help;
I hope in Your Word.
My eyes are awake through the night watches,
That I may **meditate** on Your Word.
Hear my voice according to Your lovingkindness;
O Lord, revive me according to Your justice.
They draw near who follow after wickedness;
They are far from Your law.
You are near, O Lord,
And all Your commandments are Truth.
Concerning Your testimonies, I have known of old that
You have founded them forever.

24/7 Prayer

In 2005 our family moved to Southern California, this was one year after a drunk driver hit us and drove us off the road, leaving our family in devastation.

Still, in a place of recovery, I didn't know how to acclimate to such a busy lifestyle. If I went anywhere, I would be stuck in traffic for 2 or even more hours. I didn't have any close friends. Our daughters were navigating a new high school and hating their father for disrupting our lives....again.

I too was mad at my husband (and even God) for moving us to what seemed like a God forsaken land, filled with such perverseness, and compromise even in church. I didn't know how to navigate through my "new life." Then one day, I was invited to a conference in Kansas City, Missouri, (thank you Jan) it was just a weekend away. I was so desperate; I went on this adventure alone.

Once I arrived, I checked into my hotel and ventured to the conference. I found that as I stepped into the building, the Presence of the Lord was so strong; I had to go back outside and repent for my wrong attitude, and call my husband and apologize for not supporting him in our new assignment.

As I entered the place of worship and centered into the Lord, I was filled with an overwhelming sense of peace. When the main speaker opened his mouth, the first thing he spoke was, "We need to stand in the gap for California!" God took me all the way to Missouri to pray for California. He spoke the very words that my husband had been telling me.

"We need to stand in the gap and pray for California so that God's judgment against it would be held back."

As I traveled back to California that following week, I had such a desire to create an atmosphere of prayer like that in Kansas City, Missouri. I believed for the same type of conviction that came to me when I entered their campus. So I submitted the desire of praying 24 hours a day, seven days a week, to my husband. His response was, "Tonja, they don't know how to pray for one hour, how can they pray 24/7?"

Since that day, we started a journey towards teaching God's people to pray at The Gathering at Corona, California. We have consistently scheduled prayer. We do not have a 24/7 house of prayer, but we have a people committed to praying continually. We have been in Southern California now for 12 years, and God has stayed the judgment on our land!

Supporting Scriptures

Psalm 5:3 *My voice You shall hear in the morning, O Lord; in the morning I will direct it to You, and I will look up.*

Psalm 63:1-8 *O God, You are my God; early will I seek You; My soul thirsts for You; my flesh longs for You in a dry and thirsty land where there is no water. So, I have looked for You in the sanctuary, to see Your power and Your glory. Because Your lovingkindness is better than life, my lips shall praise You. Thus, I will bless You while I live; I will lift up my hands in Your Name. My soul shall be satisfied as with marrow and fatness, and my mouth shall praise You with joyful lips. When I remember You on my bed, I meditate on You in the night watches. Because You have been my help, therefore in the shadow of Your wings I will rejoice. My soul follows close behind You; Your right hand upholds me.*

Psalm 145:18-21 *The Lord is near to all who call upon Him, to all who call upon Him in Truth. He will fulfill the desire of those who fear Him; He also will hear their cry and save them. The Lord preserves all who love Him, but all the wicked He will destroy. My mouth shall speak the praise of the Lord, and all flesh shall bless His holy Name forever and ever.*

Luke 21:33 *Heaven and earth will pass away, but My Words will by no means pass away.*

Key Word Definition

Meditate:
1) To dwell on anything in thought; to contemplate; to study; to turn or revolve any subject in the mind, appropriately but not exclusively used of pious contemplation, or a consideration of the great truths of religion.

2) To intend; to have contemplation.

Ps. 1:2 His delight is in the law of the Lord, and in His law doth he *meditate* day and night.

Meditate:
1) To plan by revolving in the mind; to contrive; to intend.

2) To think on; to revolve in the mind.

Strong's Definition: H7878 see'-akh A primitive root; to ponder, that is, (by implication) converse (with oneself, and hence aloud) or (transitively) utter: - **commune**, complain, declare, meditate, muse, pray, speak, talk (with).

Total KJV Occurrences: 20

Time of Reflection

What needs to change about my thought life?

_____
_____
_____
_____
_____
_____
_____
_____
_____
_____
_____

Prayer to Change my Mind (thinking)

Father, I ask You today, that You would help me to meditate on good things. Help me to see myself, and others through the Truth of Your Word. I ask that You help me to see the area's that I need to change the way I think. Give me Your Truth to displace every lie that I have believed, in the power of Your Name, Jesus. **John 14:6**

DAY 20

The Entirety of Your
Word is Truth

Psalm 119:153-161
RESH
(Pronounced REHSH or REYSH)

Consider my affliction and deliver me,
for I do not forget Your law.
Plead my cause and redeem me;
Revive me according to Your Word.
Salvation is far from the wicked,
For they do not seek Your statutes.
Great are Your tender mercies, O Lord;
Revive me according to Your judgments.
Many are my persecutors and my enemies,
Yet I do not turn from Your testimonies.
I see the treacherous, and am disgusted,
Because they do not keep Your Word.
Consider how I love Your precepts;
Revive me, O Lord, according to Your lovingkindness.
The entirety of Your Word is Truth,
And everyone of Your righteous judgments endures
forever.

Finding Freedom & Building Lives

There were so many challenges I faced in preparing for our move from Michigan back to California! The thought of being a part of another church denomination pained my heart. Just thinking of the rejection our family had encountered before was the last thing in the world that I wanted to embrace, nor see our daughters have to go through that kind of pain again.

Then one day, the Holy Spirit spoke to me and reminded me of a movie that I had seen years before, "Matrix." At the end of this movie, Neo recognizes his authority, and the agents that were chasing him no longer had power over him. Neo then runs at Agent Smith and destroys him from the inside out, as incredible beams of light explode the agent like a sunburst discharging. At that moment, I realized the religious spirit would NOT have authority over me, but that we would be able to go into it, and change it from the inside out.

Well, 2 years later, we were faced with the denomination not wanting us there (Go figure). But the difference this time was, that even though a FEW leaders didn't want us, the majority of the congregation did.

We prayed about leaving the region to find out what the Lord had for us. This time was unlike the last. The Lord spoke to my husband and said, "I sent you to this region to pastor these people." So that's what we did! This was the day we were delivered from every fear of man and chose to follow the Lord in the face of uncertainty. We were able to start our own church, and named it, Thegathering@corona. We are now ten years later, and we now have a network of Gathering churches, **finding freedom and building lives!**

Supporting Scriptures

1 Samuel 24:8-12 David also arose afterward, went out of the cave, and called out to Saul, saying, "My lord the king!" And when Saul looked behind him, David stooped with his face to the earth, and bowed down. And David said to Saul; "Why do you listen to the words of men who say, 'Indeed David seeks your harm? Look, this day your eyes have seen that the Lord delivered you today into my hand in the cave, and someone urged me to kill you. But my eye spared you, and I said, 'I will not stretch out my hand against my lord, for he is the Lord's anointed.' Moreover, my father, see! Yes, see the corner of your robe in my hand! For in that I cut off the corner of your robe, and did not kill you, know and see that there is neither evil nor rebellion in my hand, and I have not sinned against you. Yet you hunt my life to take it. Therefore let the Lord be judge, and judge between you and me, and see and plead my case, and deliver me out of your hand."

Micah 7:5-9 Do not trust in a friend; do not put your confidence in a companion; guard the doors of your mouth from her who lies in your bosom. For son dishonors father, daughter rises against her mother, daughter-in-law against her mother-in-law; a man's enemies are the men of his own household. Therefore I will look to the Lord; I will wait for the God of my salvation; My God will hear me. Do not rejoice over me, my enemy; when I fall, I will arise; when I sit in darkness, the Lord will be a light to me. I will bear the indignation of the Lord, because I have sinned against Him, until He pleads my case and executes justice for me. He will bring me forth to the light; I will see His righteousness.

Psalm 44:18 Our heart has not turned back, nor have our steps departed from Your way.

Ezekiel 9:4 And the Lord said to him, "Go through the midst of the city, through the midst of Jerusalem, and put a mark on the foreheads of the men who sigh and cry over all the abominations that are done within it."

Key Word Definition

Truth: Conformity to fact or reality; exact accordance with that which is, or has been, or shall be. The truth of history constitutes its whole value. We rely on the truth of the scriptural prophecies. Proverbs 8: My mouth shall speak truth...... John 17 Thy Word is truth.....

Strong's Concordance: True: <u>H571</u> eh'-meth Contracted from <u>H539</u>; stability; figuratively certainty, truth, trustworthiness: - assured (-ly), establishment, faithful, right, sure, true (-ly, -th), verity.

Total KJV Occurrences: 127

Time of Reflection

Has there been a time that you experienced a betrayal? Search out the scriptures on how Jesus and others responded to betrayal.

_____
_____
_____
_____
_____
_____
_____
_____
_____
_____
_____
_____

A Thankful Prayer

I thank You, Father, that Your Word is Truth, and I can trust what You have said. Help me to determine Satan's lies and to find the Truth of what You are saying in every situation! I break the agreement with every generational curse that was handed to me by my ancestors, by the power of the shed blood that Jesus shed on the cross for me. I choose to forgive and forgive again every offense and curse that was handed to me by the generations before me. I thank You, Lord, for your grace and ability to accomplish all that You have for me by Your precious Spirit. In the mighty Name of Your Son Jesus! **Exodus 20:5**

DAY 21

Great Peace to Those Who Love Your Law

Psalm 119:161-168
SHIN
(Pronounced SHEEN)

Princes persecute me without a cause,
But my heart stands in awe of Your Word.
I rejoice at Your Word
As one who finds great treasure.
I hate and abhor lying,
But I love Your law,
Seven times a day I praise You,
Because of Your righteous judgments.
Great peace have those who love Your law,
And nothing causes them to stumble,
Lord, I hope for Your salvation,
And I do Your commandments.
My soul keeps Your testimonies,
And I love them exceedingly.
I keep Your precepts and Your testimonies,
For all my ways are before You.

113

The Ancient of Days
May 3, 2015

I was on my face one Sunday after Apostle Isaac Ramirez preached to the Gathering at Corona, California. I had been crying with everything within me for this next move of God! That an actual reforming would take place and that we would be those that would truly embrace ALL that God has for us, with NO traces of a Religious spirit. A people entirely free to be All that we were created for. Just when I didn't think I could cry anymore, I started having an open vision as I was caught up in the Spirit. I was completely disconnected from everything that was going on around me naturally,

The Ancient of Days came to me. He was all in white and surrounded with this beautiful Glory covered in gold. It was so bright and consuming that as soon as He picked me up, I was covered with the same glorious gold. His hair was white and long, He had this consuming fire in His eyes that appeared like an ocean, a fiery red and midnight blue ocean. The depth was so amazingly deep, it was as if I could walk into His eyes and step upon the seas.

He picked my limp body up and carried me to the Throne and sat me on His Fathers lap. I grabbed him like a little girl would grab her daddies neck, and He held me like a mother would hold a newborn child. I looked into His face, and it was the face of a Lion, with Consuming Fire in His Eyes. Immediately, He stood me up right in front of Him, (facing outward). As soon as He stood me up, I was overwhelmed with arrows coming at me from all sides. It seemed like 100's of them all at once. As I looked to see where they were coming from, I saw that they were coming from our very own congregation of people. So many thoughts rushed through my mind all at once. I couldn't understand why God put me in front of all of these arrows. Why wasn't HE protecting me?

Immediately, my right arm went up and caught every arrow, and I was able to shoot them back to where they were coming from. With one exception, the arrows that I was shooting back towards every person that originally shot them at me, was taking out the demon that was standing behind the individuals, that was influencing them.

The Lord spoke this word following the vision:

The Glory of God is rising in this hour to reveal, to heal, and to restore the broken hearted. But we must be found in the arms of the Father. In that place, the Ancient of Days, the Lion of the tribe of Judah will arm you with strength. He's arming us in this hour with the strength from the Most High, to take out the enemies and not each other. God is turning us in this hour to no longer fight each other, but to take out the enemies that are influencing. The Lord says I am revealing My heart in this hour, I am arming My sons and daughters with weapons of war and weapons of love.

Supporting Scriptures

Proverbs 3:1-6 *My son, do not forget my law, but let your heart keep my commands; for length of days and long life and peace they will add to you. Let not mercy and truth forsake you; bind them around your neck, write them on the tablet of your heart, and so find favor and high esteem in the sight of God and man. Trust in the Lord with all your heart, and lean not on your own understanding; in all your ways acknowledge Him, and He shall direct your paths. Do not be wise in your own eyes; Fear the Lord and depart from evil. I will be health to your flesh, and strength to your bones.*

Isaiah 26:3 *You will keep him in perfect peace, whose mind is stayed on You, because he trusts in You.*

Isaiah 32:17-18 *The work of righteousness will be peace, and the effect of righteousness, quietness and assurance forever. My people will dwell in a peaceful habitation, in secure dwellings, and in quiet resting places.*

Key Word Definition

Peace:
1) In a general sense, a state of quiet or tranquility; freedom from disturbance or agitation; applicable to society, to individuals, or to the temper of mind.

2) Freedom from war with a foreign nation; public quiet.

3) Freedom from internal commotion or civil war.

4) Freedom from private quarrels, suits or disturbance.

5) Freedom from agitation or disturbance by the passions, as from fear, terror, anger, anxiety or the like; quietness of mind; tranquility; calmness; quiet of conscience. Psalm 119 Great peace have they that love your law.

6) Heavenly rest; the happiness of heaven. Isaiah 57

7) Harmony; concord; a state of reconciliation between parties a variance.

8) Public tranquility; that quiet order and security which is guaranteed by laws; as to keep the peace, to break the peace.
      This word is used in commanding silence or quiet, as, peace to this troubled soul.

> *Peace*, the lovers are asleep.
> *Crashau*

To be at peace, to be reconciled; to live in harmony;

To make peace to reconcile, as parties at variance.

To hold the peace; To be silent; to suppress one's thoughts; not to speak.

Strong's Concordance: H7965 shaw-lome', shaw-lome' From H7999 safe, that is, (figuratively) well, happy, friendly; also (abstractly) welfare, that is, health, (X perfect, such as be at) peace (-able, -ably), prosper (-ity, -ous), rest, safe (-ly), salute, welfare, (X all is, be) well, X wholly.

Total KJV Occurrences: 236

Time of Reflection

Identify the areas that you need peace.

Take the time just as David did in this Psalm to praise the Lord seven times throughout your day. Receive God's peace as you praise Him!

At the end of your day, assess the process of receiving peace.

_____

_____

_____

_____

_____

_____

_____

_____

_____

_____

_____

Prayer for Peace

Father, I ask that You forgive me for not allowing Your peace to guide me. Today, I choose to submit myself to You. I also choose to be directed by the peace that comes from You, Your Word, and from that place of worship with just You and I. You said You are not the author of confusion. So I thank You that in every place of confusion that You would help me to find that stillness that comes from Your presence and brings peace. In the mighty Name of Jesus Christ, Amen! **Isaiah 26:3**

DAY 22

Deliver Me
According to Your Word

Psalm 119:169–176
TAU
(Pronounced TAHV or TAHF)

Let my cry come before You, O Lord,
Give me understanding according to Your Word.
Let my supplication come before You;
Deliver me according to Your Word.
My lips shall utter praise,
For You teach me Your statutes.
My tongue shall speak of Your Word,
For all Your commandments are righteousness.
Let Your hand become my help,
For I have chosen Your precepts.
I long for Your salvation,
O Lord, and Your law is my delight.
Let my soul live, and it shall praise You;
And let Your judgments help me.
I have gone astray like a lost sheep;
Seek Your servant, for I do not forget Your
commandments.

Vision and Prophecy of
Two Doors
May 5, 2015

There are two doors placed before us, one is a fiery door, and the second a whitewashed door. The fiery door will give you access to the Father, it will take you through the purification process and purge you with hyssop. There will be many trials and tribulations through this door. But the one thing that will remain, will be the Love of The Father. The heart of the One true lover of our souls. Our friend Jesus will be with us in this fire, for He is our access point. The only way to the Father is through the Son. Shadrach, Meshach, and Abednego were delivered to the furnace of fire, but they were not burned, for the Lord of the Most High was with them in the flames.

The white-washed door has a cliff right as you enter. It leads to the gates of hell. This door is very difficult to get through, and it stands before the fiery door, many cry out and say this is the way to go. They make many plans, meetings, and counseling sessions to help prepare people for this door. They have rules, regulations and many laws, burdens, and yokes that they place on people to get through the door. They even say this is the way to heaven. But they don't know that where they are going, is not heaven. They are leading their flocks through the wrong door!

Why are they going through the wrong door? It's because they are filled with fear and are more concerned with filling their own treasuries rather than Mine, says the Lord. They don't know that the day is coming that I will require an account for all they have done, and not done. When I told them to feed My sheep, they ate till their bellies were full. When I told them to clothe the naked, they clothed

120

themselves with jewels and glamor to be seen by men. When I told them to sell all that they had and follow Me. They were filled with every kind of fear and said that I was very difficult to follow.

I require an opening of the books at My appearing, I will require that all give an account. It is in this hour you are given an opportunity. It is in this hour you are given a choice. Will you be those that will choose to save your own soul, and let those around you suffer in hunger, being poor and naked? Will you lay down your life for mine? Will you take up your cross and follow Me?

I desire you to break through the lies that the Pharisee spirit tries to clothe My Bride with. I desire you to come to Me and find rest. I will give you peace. I will bring you to the place of My bosom, says the Lord.

You are Mine, and I am yours. I purchased you with My very own blood. I made a way where there seems to be no way. Come, come, come to Me and I will lead you into complete Truth. I will lead you to the Desire of all Nations, I will cover you, and I will keep you. Even though you pass through many waters, they will not overtake you, even though you walk through the fire, you will not be burned. IAM a covenant keeping Father, I will not let you be overtaken by the enemy of your souls. I will not let you fall by the wayside.

Stay close to Me, and My heart and you will see that I will cover you completely. Let go of everything that tries to hold you back. Draw near to Me, and I will draw near to you, and deliver you in times of famine, disaster, and every form of trouble. It is in My heart that you find the safety you yearn for.

Supporting Scriptures

*Psalm 119:27 Make me understand the way of Your precepts; So shall I **meditate** on Your wonderful works.*

Psalm 119:144 The righteousness of Your testimonies is everlasting; Give me understanding, and I shall live.

Joshua 24:21-24 And the people said to Joshua, "No, but we will serve the Lord!" So Joshua said to the people, "You are a witness against yourselves that you have chosen the Lord for yourselves, to serve Him." And they said we are witnesses!" "Now therefore," he said, "put away the foreign gods which are among you, and incline your heart to the Lord God of Israel." And the people said to Joshua, "The Lord our God we will serve, and His voice we will obey!"

Psalm 119: 16 I will delight myself in Your statutes; I will not forget Your Word.

Isaiah 53:4-8 Surely He has borne our griefs and carried our sorrows; yet we esteemed Him stricken, smitten by God, and afflicted. But He was wounded for our transgressions, He was bruised for our iniquities; the chastisement for our peace was upon Him, and by His stripes we are healed. All we like sheep have gone astray; we have turned, everyone, to his own way; And the Lord has laid on Him the iniquity of us all. He was oppressed and He was afflicted, yet He opened not His mouth; He was led as a lamb to the slaughter, and as a sheep before its shearers is silent, so He opened not His mouth. He was taken from prison and from judgment, and who will declare His generation? For He was cut off from the land of the living; for the transgressions of My people He was stricken.

Key Word Definition

Deliver:
1) To free; to release, as from restaint; to set at liberty, as, to deliver one from captivity.

2) To rescue, or save.

3) To give, or transfer; to put into another's hand or power; to commit; to pass from one to another.

4) To surrender; to yield; to give up; to resign; as, to deliver a frotress to an enemy. It is often follwed up by; as, to deliver up the city; to deliver up stolen goods.

Strong's Concordance H5337 A primitive root; to snatch away, whether in a good or a bad sense: - X at all, defend, deliver (self), escape, X without fail, part, pluck, preserve, recover, rescue, rid, save, spoil, strip, X surely, take (out).

Total KJV occurrences: 213

Time of Reflection

Are there areas that I need to release and surrender to the Lord? Take the time, and release each place to Him.

_____

_____

_____

_____

_____

_____

_____

_____

_____

_____

Prayer of Thankfulness

I thank You, Father, that You are my deliverer, in You I put my trust! Even though I walk through difficult situations, I thank You, Lord, that You are my help in every time of need. You promised me that You would never leave me nor forsake me. I love you because you first loved me! **John 14:18**

You With Me For Eternity

It is only through Love,
And laying down your will for mine
That you become One with Me.
It is only in a perfect sacrifice
That you let go of all of yourself for Me.
You must not have selfish motives.
I must be your all-consuming passion.
I must be your first love.
In that moment you will see,
And experience Me.
Let go of all selfishness.
Let go of all the consuming thoughts
And those things of passion that are not of Me.
Then and only then will you see Me
And be one with one another,
And become One with Me, says the Lord.
Lay down your life for Mine,
And in that moment
I will be your all-consuming fire,
I will fill you with all of My desire,
With all the things that are close to my heart.
I love you with an everlasting love,
My heart burns for you,
My heart longs for you
I yearn to be with you, and you with Me,
Where I am, for Eternity!

"If You Want to Break Any Habit You Must Change and Do things Different!"

In this devotional, I have shared personal experiences, trials, traumas and testimonies of how I was able to overcome the difficulties that I faced in my life.

In Revelations 12:11 it says "And they overcame him by the blood of the Lamb and the word of their testimony; and they loved not their lives unto the death."

I have found my path to overcoming the strongholds that the enemy has thrown at me, by continually sharing my testimony every time God has brought me through a trial or a trauma. And each time I could feel the Light of God shining ever so bright into the dark places of shame, fear and all that the enemy would try to keep me bound in. It would destroy Satan's grip on my mind and also bring life and healing to others.

My prayer for you is that whatever battle you are facing that you would embrace the process of true victory through the path of God's Word. Truly hiding His Promises in your heart.

Tonja Marie Peters